Practice and Skills Fluency Workbook

Copyright © by Houghton Mifflin Harcourt Publishing Company

All rights reserved. No part of this work may be reproduced or transmitted in any form or by any means, electronic or mechanical, including photocopying or recording, or by any information storage and retrieval system, without the prior written permission of the copyright owner unless such copying is expressly permitted by federal copyright law. Requests for permission to make copies of any part of the work should be submitted through our Permissions website at https://customercare.hmhco.com/permission/Permissions.html or mailed to Houghton Mifflin Harcourt Publishing Company, Attn: Intellectual Property Licensing, 9400 Southpark Center Loop, Orlando, Florida 32819-8647.

Printed in the U.S.A.

ISBN 978-0-544-81744-9

1 2 3 4 5 6 7 8 9 10   0928   24 23 22 21 20 19 18 17 16 15

4500571513   A B C D E F G

If you have received these materials as examination copies free of charge, Houghton Mifflin Harcourt Publishing Company retains title to the materials and they may not be resold. Resale of examination copies is strictly prohibited.

Possession of this publication in print format does not entitle users to convert this publication, or any portion of it, into electronic format.

Contents

Student Worksheets

Module 1 Real Numbers

Lesson 1-1
Practice and Problem Solving: A/B 1
Reteach 2

Lesson 1-2
Practice and Problem Solving: A/B 3
Reteach 4

Lesson 1-3
Practice and Problem Solving: A/B 5
Reteach 6

Module 2 Exponents and Scientific Notation

Lesson 2-1
Practice and Problem Solving: A/B 7
Reteach 8

Lesson 2-2
Practice and Problem Solving: A/B 9
Reteach 10

Lesson 2-3
Practice and Problem Solving: A/B 11
Reteach 12

Lesson 2-4
Practice and Problem Solving: A/B 13
Reteach 14

Module 3 Proportional Relationships

Lesson 3-1
Practice and Problem Solving: A/B 15
Reteach 16

Lesson 3-2
Practice and Problem Solving: A/B 17
Reteach 18

Lesson 3-3
Practice and Problem Solving: A/B 19
Reteach 20

Module 4 Nonproportional Relationships

Lesson 4-1
Practice and Problem Solving: A/B 21
Reteach 22

Lesson 4-2
Practice and Problem Solving: A/B 23
Reteach 24

Lesson 4-3
Practice and Problem Solving: A/B 25
Reteach 26

Lesson 4-4
Practice and Problem Solving: A/B 27
Reteach 28

Module 5 Writing Linear Equations

Lesson 5-1
Practice and Problem Solving: A/B 29
Reteach 30

Lesson 5-2
Practice and Problem Solving: A/B 31
Reteach 32

Lesson 5-3
Practice and Problem Solving: A/B 33
Reteach 34

Module 6 Functions

Lesson 6-1
Practice and Problem Solving: A/B 35
Reteach 36

Lesson 6-2
Practice and Problem Solving: A/B 37
Reteach 38

Lesson 6-3
Practice and Problem Solving: A/B 39
Reteach 40

Lesson 6-4
Practice and Problem Solving: A/B 41
Reteach 42

Original content Copyright © by Houghton Mifflin Harcourt. Additions and changes to the original content are the responsibility of the instructor.

Module 7 Solving Linear Equations

Lesson 7-1
Practice and Problem Solving: A/B 43
Reteach 44

Lesson 7-2
Practice and Problem Solving: A/B 45
Reteach 46

Lesson 7-3
Practice and Problem Solving: A/B 47
Reteach 48

Lesson 7-4
Practice and Problem Solving: A/B 49
Reteach 50

Module 8 Solving Systems of Linear Equations

Lesson 8-1
Practice and Problem Solving: A/B 51
Reteach 52

Lesson 8-2
Practice and Problem Solving: A/B 53
Reteach 54

Lesson 8-3
Practice and Problem Solving: A/B 55
Reteach 56

Lesson 8-4
Practice and Problem Solving: A/B 57
Reteach 58

Lesson 8-5
Practice and Problem Solving: A/B 59
Reteach 60

Module 9 Transformations and Congruence

Lesson 9-1
Practice and Problem Solving: A/B 61
Reteach 62

Lesson 9-2
Practice and Problem Solving: A/B 63
Reteach 64

Lesson 9-3
Practice and Problem Solving: A/B 65
Reteach 66

Lesson 9-4
Practice and Problem Solving: A/B 67
Reteach 68

Lesson 9-5
Practice and Problem Solving: A/B 69
Reteach 70

Module 10 Transformations and Similarity

Lesson 10-1
Practice and Problem Solving: A/B 71
Reteach 72

Lesson 10-2
Practice and Problem Solving: A/B 73
Reteach 74

Lesson 10-3
Practice and Problem Solving: A/B 75
Reteach 76

Module 11 Angle Relationships in Parallel Lines and Triangles

Lesson 11-1
Practice and Problem Solving: A/B 77
Reteach 78

Lesson 11-2
Practice and Problem Solving: A/B 79
Reteach 80

Lesson 11-3
Practice and Problem Solving: A/B 81
Reteach 82

Module 12 The Pythagorean Theorem

Lesson 12-1
Practice and Problem Solving: A/B 83
Reteach 84

Lesson 12-2
Practice and Problem Solving: A/B 85
Reteach 86

Original content Copyright © by Houghton Mifflin Harcourt. Additions and changes to the original content are the responsibility of the instructor.

Lesson 12-3
Practice and Problem Solving: A/B 87
Reteach 88

Module 13   Volume

Lesson 13-1
Practice and Problem Solving: A/B 89
Reteach 90

Lesson 13-2
Practice and Problem Solving: A/B 91
Reteach 92

Lesson 13-3
Practice and Problem Solving: A/B 93
Reteach 94

Module 14   Scatter Plots

Lesson 14-1
Practice and Problem Solving: A/B 95
Reteach 96

Lesson 14-2
Practice and Problem Solving: A/B 97
Reteach 98

Module 15   Two-Way Tables

Lesson 15-1
Practice and Problem Solving: A/B 99
Reteach 100

Lesson 15-2
Practice and Problem Solving: A/B 101
Reteach 102

Name _____ Date _____ Class _____

LESSON 1-1 Rational and Irrational Numbers
Practice and Problem Solving: A/B

Write each fraction as a decimal.

1. $\frac{1}{8}$　　　2. $\frac{9}{16}$　　　3. $\frac{11}{20}$　　　4. $5\frac{8}{25}$

_____　　_____　　_____　　_____

5. $\frac{14}{15}$　　　6. $2\frac{7}{12}$　　　7. $\frac{3}{100}$　　　8. $\frac{16}{5}$

_____　　_____　　_____　　_____

Find the two square roots of each number.

9. 25　　　10. 1　　　11. $\frac{25}{4}$　　　12. $\frac{121}{49}$

_____　　_____　　_____　　_____

Find the cube root of each number.

13. 8　　　14. 216　　　15. 1　　　16. 2197

_____　　_____　　_____　　_____

Approximate each irrational number to the nearest hundredth without using a calculator.

17. $\sqrt{32}$　　　18. $\sqrt{118}$　　　19. $\sqrt{18}$　　　20. $\sqrt{319}$

_____　　_____　　_____　　_____

Approximate each irrational number to the nearest hundredth without using a calculator. Then plot each number on a number line.

21. $\sqrt{8}$ _____　　　　22. $\sqrt{75}$ _____

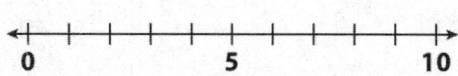

23. A tablet weighs 1.23 pounds. What is its weight written as a mixed number?

_____

24. The area of a square mirror is 256 in². A rectangular mirror has a width the same as the square mirror's width. Its length is two inches longer than its width. What is the area of the rectangular mirror?

_____

Original content Copyright © by Houghton Mifflin Harcourt. Additions and changes to the original content are the responsibility of the instructor.

Name _____ Date _____ Class _____

LESSON 1-1 Rational and Irrational Numbers
Reteach

To write a fraction as a decimal, divide the numerator by the denominator.

A decimal may terminate.

$$\frac{3}{4} = 4\overline{)3.00} = 0.75$$
$$-28\downarrow$$
$$20$$
$$-20$$
$$0$$

A decimal may repeat.

$$\frac{1}{3} = 3\overline{)1.00} = 0.\overline{3}$$
$$-9\downarrow$$
$$10$$
$$-9$$
$$1$$

Complete to write each fraction as a decimal.

1. $\frac{15}{4} = 4\overline{)15.00}$

2. $\frac{5}{6} = 6\overline{)5.00}$

3. $\frac{11}{3} = 3\overline{)11.00}$

Every positive number has two square roots, one positive and one negative.

Since $5 \times 5 = 25$ and also $-5 \times -5 = 25$, both 5 and -5 are square roots of 25.

$\sqrt{25} = 5$ and $-\sqrt{25} = -5$

Every positive number has one cube root.
Since $4 \times 4 \times 4 = 64$, 4 is the cube root of 64.

Find the two square roots for each number.

4. 81

5. 49

6. $\frac{25}{36}$

_____ _____ _____

Find the cube root for each number.

7. 27

8. 125

9. 729

_____ _____ _____

LESSON 1-2: Sets of Real Numbers

Practice and Problem Solving: A/B

List all number sets that apply to each number.

1. $-\dfrac{4}{5}$

2. $\sqrt{15}$

3. -2

4. -25

5. $0.\overline{3}$

6. $\dfrac{20}{4}$

Tell whether the given statement is true or false. Explain your choice.

7. All real numbers are rational.

8. All whole numbers are integers.

Identify the set of numbers that best describes each situation. Explain your choice.

9. the amount of money in a bank account

10. the exact temperature of a glass of water in degrees Celsius

Place each number in the correct location on the Venn diagram.

11. $-\dfrac{5}{9}$

12. $-\sqrt{100}$

13. π

14. $\sqrt{25}$

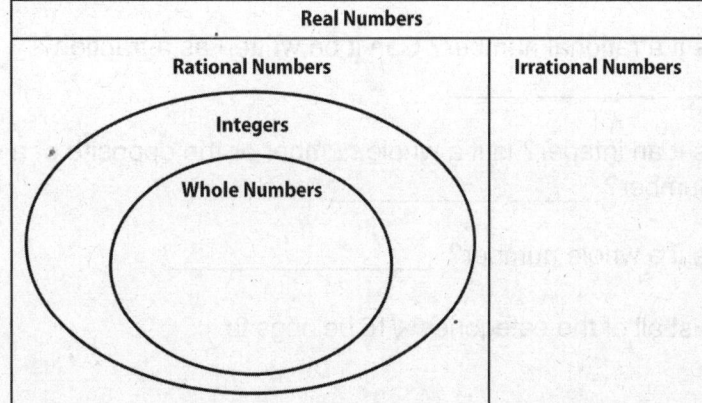

Name _____ Date _____ Class _____

LESSON 1-2
Sets of Real Numbers
Reteach

Numbers can be organized into groups. Each number can be placed into one or more of the groups.

Real numbers include all rational and irrational numbers. All of the numbers that we use in everyday life are real numbers.

- If a real number can be written as a fraction, it is a **rational number**. If it cannot be written as a fraction, it is an **irrational number**.
- If a rational number is a whole number, or the opposite of a whole number, then it is an **integer**.
- If an integer is positive or 0, then it is a **whole number**.

You can use these facts to categorize any number.

A. What kind of number is 10?

Is it a real number? *Yes.*

Is it a rational number? Can it be written as a fraction? *Yes:* $\frac{10}{1}$

Is it an integer? Is it a whole number or the opposite of a whole number? *Yes.*

Is it a whole number? *Yes.*

So 10 is a real number, a rational number, an integer, and a whole number.

B. What kind of number is $\sqrt{\frac{9}{3}}$?

Is it a real number? *Yes.*

Is it a rational number? Can it be written as a fraction? *No.* $\frac{9}{3}$ *simplifies to 3. If you try to find the square root of 3, you will get a decimal answer that goes on forever but does not repeat: 1.7320508… This cannot be written as a fraction.*

So $\sqrt{\frac{9}{3}}$ is a real, irrational number.

Answer each question to identify the categories the given number belongs to.

$\sqrt{16}$

1. Is it a real number? _____

2. Is it a rational number? Can it be written as a fraction?
_____

3. Is it an integer? Is it a whole number or the opposite of a whole number? _____

4. Is it a whole number? _____

5. List all of the categories $\sqrt{16}$ belongs to.
_____

Name _____ Date _____ Class _____

LESSON 1-3 Ordering Real Numbers
Practice and Problem Solving: A/B

Compare. Write <, >, or = .

1. $\sqrt{5} + 3 \bigcirc \sqrt{5} + 4$
2. $\sqrt{6} + 13 \bigcirc \sqrt{10} + 13$
3. $\sqrt{7} + 4 \bigcirc 5 + \sqrt{6}$
4. $8 + \sqrt{2} \bigcirc \sqrt{8} + 2$
5. $3 + \sqrt{3} \bigcirc \sqrt{13} - 7$
6. $11 - \sqrt{3} \bigcirc 5 - \sqrt{3}$

Use the table to answer the questions.

7. List the butterflies in order from greatest to least wingspan.

_____
_____
_____
_____

Butterfly	Wingspan (in.)
Great white	3.75
Large orange sulphur	$3\frac{3}{8}$
Apricot sulphur	2.625
White-angled sulphur	3.5

8. The pink-spotted swallowtail's wingspan can measure $3\frac{5}{16}$ inches.

   Between which two butterflies should the pink-spotted swallowtail be in your list from question 7?

   _____

Order each group of numbers from least to greatest.

9. $\sqrt{8}, 2, \frac{\sqrt{7}}{2}$

10. $\sqrt{12}, \pi, 3.5$

_____
_____

11. $\sqrt{26}, -20, 13.5, \sqrt{35}$

12. $\sqrt{6}, -5.25, \frac{3}{2}, 5$

_____
_____

Solve.

13. Four people have used different methods to find the height of a wall. Their results are shown in the table. Order their measurements from greatest to least. $\pi \approx 3.14$

Wall Height (m)			
Allie	Byron	Justin	Rosa
$\sqrt{12} - 1$	$\frac{5}{2}$	2.25	$1 + \frac{\pi}{2}$

_____

Original content Copyright © by Houghton Mifflin Harcourt. Additions and changes to the original content are the responsibility of the instructor.

LESSON 1-3 Ordering Real Numbers
Reteach

Compare and order real numbers from least to greatest.

Order $\sqrt{22}$, $\pi + 1$, and $4\frac{1}{2}$ from least to greatest.

You can use a calculator to approximate irrational numbers.

$\sqrt{22} \approx 4.69$

You know that $\pi \approx 3.14$, so you can find the approximate value of $\pi + 1$.

$\pi + 1 \approx 3.14 + 1 \approx 4.14$

Plot $\sqrt{22}$, $\pi + 1$, and $4\frac{1}{2}$ on a number line.

On a number line, the values of numbers increase as you move from left to right. So, to order these numbers from least to greatest, list them from left to right.

$\pi + 1$, $4\frac{1}{2}$, and $\sqrt{22}$

Order each group of numbers from least to greatest.

1. 4, π, $\sqrt{8}$

2. 5, $\frac{17}{3}$, $\pi + 2$

3. $\sqrt{2}$, 1.7, -2

4. 2.5, $\sqrt{5}$, $\frac{3}{2}$

5. 3.7, $\sqrt{13}$, $\pi + 1$

6. $\frac{5}{4}$, $\pi - 2$, $\frac{\sqrt{5}}{2}$

Name _____ Date _____ Class _____

LESSON 2-1 Integer Exponents
Practice and Problem Solving: A/B

Find the value of each power.

1. $5^3 = $ _____
2. $7^{-2} = $ _____
3. $51^1 = $ _____
4. $3^{-4} = $ _____
5. $1^{12} = $ _____
6. $64^0 = $ _____
7. $4^{-3} = $ _____
8. $4^3 = $ _____
9. $10^5 = $ _____

Find the missing exponent.

10. $n^3 = n^{\square} \cdot n^{-3}$
11. $\dfrac{a^{\square}}{a^2} = a^4$
12. $(r^4)^{\square} = r^{12}$

Simplify each expression.

13. $(9-3)^2 - (5 \cdot 4)^0 = $ _____
14. $(2+3)^5 \div (5^2)^2 = $ _____
15. $4^2 \div (6-2)^4 = $ _____
16. $[(1+7)^2]^2 \cdot (12^2)^0 = $ _____

Use the description below to complete Exercises 17–20.

A shipping company makes a display to show how many cubes can fit into a large box. Each cube has sides of 2 inches. The large box has sides of 10 inches.

17. Use exponents to express the volume of each cube and the large box.

    Volume of cube = _____   Volume of large box = _____

18. Find how many cubes will fit in the box. _____

19. Suppose the shipping company were packing balls with a diameter of 2 inches instead of cubes. Would the large box hold more balls or fewer balls than boxes? Explain your answer.

    _____

    _____

20. Suppose the size of each cube is doubled and the size of the large box is doubled. How many of these new cubes will fit in that new large box? Explain how you found your answer.

    _____

Name _____ Date _____ Class _____

LESSON 2-1
Integer Exponents
Reteach

A positive exponent tells you how many times to multiply the base as a factor. A negative exponent tells you how many times to divide by the base. Any number to the 0 power is equal to 1.

$$4^2 = 4 \cdot 4 = 16 \qquad 4^5 = 4 \cdot 4 \cdot 4 \cdot 4 \cdot 4 = 1024 \qquad a^3 = a \cdot a \cdot a$$

$$4^{-2} = \frac{1}{4^2} = \frac{1}{4 \cdot 4} = \frac{1}{16} \qquad 4^{-5} = \frac{1}{4^5} = \frac{1}{4 \cdot 4 \cdot 4 \cdot 4 \cdot 4} = \frac{1}{1024} \qquad a^{-3} = \frac{1}{a^3} = \frac{1}{a \cdot a \cdot a}$$

When you work with integers, certain properties are always true. With integer exponents, there are also certain properties that are always true.

When the bases are the same and you multiply, you add exponents.

$$2^2 \cdot 2^4 = 2^{2+4}$$
$$\underbrace{2 \cdot 2} \cdot \underbrace{2 \cdot 2 \cdot 2 \cdot 2} = 2^6 \qquad a^m \cdot a^n = a^{m+n}$$

When the bases are the same and you divide, you subtract exponents.

$$\frac{2^5}{2^3} = 2^{5-3}$$

$$\frac{2 \cdot 2 \cdot \cancel{2} \cdot \cancel{2} \cdot \cancel{2}}{\cancel{2} \cdot \cancel{2} \cdot \cancel{2}} = 2^2 \qquad \frac{a^m}{a^n} = a^{m-n}$$

When you raise a power to a power, you multiply.

$$(2^3)^2 = 2^{3 \cdot 2}$$
$$(2 \cdot 2 \cdot 2)^2$$
$$(2 \cdot 2 \cdot 2) \cdot (2 \cdot 2 \cdot 2) = 2^6 \qquad (a^m)^n = a^{m \cdot n}$$

Tell whether you will add, subtract, or multiply the exponents. Then simplify by finding the value of the expression.

1. $\dfrac{3^6}{3^3} \rightarrow$ _____

2. $8^2 \cdot 8^{-3} \rightarrow$ _____

3. $(3^2)^3 \rightarrow$ _____

4. $5^3 \cdot 5^1 \rightarrow$ _____

5. $\dfrac{4^2}{4^4} \rightarrow$ _____

6. $(6^2)^2 \rightarrow$ _____

Original content Copyright © by Houghton Mifflin Harcourt. Additions and changes to the original content are the responsibility of the instructor.

Name _____ Date _____ Class _____

LESSON 2-2
Scientific Notation with Positive Powers of 10
Practice and Problem Solving: A/B

Write each number as a power of 10.

1. 100
2. 10,000
3. 100,000
4. 10,000,000

5. 1,000,000
6. 1000
7. 1,000,000,000
8. 1

Write each power of ten in standard notation.

9. 10^3
10. 10^5
11. 10
12. 10^6

13. 10^2
14. 10^0
15. 10^4
16. 10^7

Write each number in scientific notation.

17. 2500
18. 300
19. 47,300
20. 24

21. 14,565
22. 7001
23. 19,050,000
24. 33

Write each number in standard notation.

25. 6×10^3
26. 4.5×10^2
27. 7×10^7
28. 1.05×10^4

29. 3.052×10^3
30. 5×10^0
31. 9.87×10^1
32. 5.43×10^1

Solve.

33. The average distance of the Moon from Earth is about 384,400 kilometers. Write this number in scientific notation.

34. The radius of Earth is about 6.38×10^3 kilometers. Write this distance in standard notation.

Name _____ Date _____ Class _____

Scientific Notation with Positive Powers of 10
Reteach

You can change a number from standard notation to scientific notation in 3 steps.
1. Place the decimal point between the first and second digits on the left to make a number between 1 and 10.
2. Count from the decimal point to the right of the last digit on the right.
3. Use the number of places counted in Step 2 as the power of ten.

Example
Write 125,000 in scientific notation.

1.25
125,000
1.25×10^5

1) The first and second digits to the left are 1 and 2, so place the decimal point between the two digits to make the number 1.25.
2) The last digit in 125,000 is 5 places to the right.
3) The power of 10 is 5.

You can change a number from scientific notation to standard notation in 3 steps.
1. Find the power of 10.
2. Count that number of places to the right.
3. Add zeros as needed.

Example
Write 5.96×10^4 in standard notation.

10^4
5.9600
59,600

1) The power of 10 is 4.
2) Move the decimal point 4 places to the right.
3) Add two zeros.

Complete to write each number in scientific notation.

1. 34,600

   The number between 1 and 10: ____

   The power of 10: ____

   The number in scientific notation:

   _____

2. 1,050,200

   The number between 1 and 10: ____

   The power of 10: ____

   The number in scientific notation:

   _____

Write each number in standard notation.

3. 1.057×10^3

4. 3×10^8

5. 5.24×10^5

_____   _____   _____

Original content Copyright © by Houghton Mifflin Harcourt. Additions and changes to the original content are the responsibility of the instructor.

LESSON 2-3

Scientific Notation with Negative Powers of 10
Practice and Problem Solving: A/B

Write each number as a negative power of ten.

1. $\frac{1}{10^2} = $ _____
2. $\frac{1}{10^4} = $ _____
3. $\frac{1}{10^5} = $ _____
4. $\frac{1}{10^7} = $ _____

5. $\frac{1}{10^6} = $ _____
6. $\frac{1}{10^3} = $ _____
7. $\frac{1}{10^9} = $ _____
8. $\frac{1}{10^1} = $ _____

Write each power of ten in standard notation.

9. $10^{-3} = $ _____
10. $10^{-5} = $ _____
11. $10^{-1} = $ _____
12. $10^{-6} = $ _____

13. $10^{-2} = $ _____
14. $10^{-9} = $ _____
15. $10^{-4} = $ _____
16. $10^{-7} = $ _____

Write each number in scientific notation.

17. 0.025
18. 0.3
19. 0.000473
20. 0.0024

21. 0.000014565
22. 0.70010
23. 0.0190500
24. 0.00330000

Write each number in standard notation.

25. 6×10^{-3}
26. 4.5×10^{-2}
27. 7×10^{-7}
28. 1.05×10^{-6}

29. 3.052×10^{-8}
30. 5×10^{-1}
31. 9.87×10^{-4}
32. 5.43×10^{-5}

Solve.

33. An *E. coli* bacterium has a diameter of about 5×10^{-7} meter. Write this measurement as a decimal in standard notation.

34. A human hair has an average diameter of about 0.000017 meter. Write this measurement in scientific notation.

Name _____ Date _____ Class _____

LESSON 2-3 Scientific Notation with Negative Powers of 10
Reteach

You can convert a number from standard form to scientific notation in 3 steps.
1. Starting from the left, find the first non-zero digit. To the right of this digit is the new location of your decimal point.
2. Count the number of places you moved the decimal point. This number will be used in the exponent in the power of ten.
3. Since the original decimal value was less than 1, your power of ten must be negative. Place a negative sign in front of the exponent.

Example
Write 0.00496 in standard notation.

4.96	1)	The first non-zero digit is 4, so move the decimal point to the right of the 4.
4.96×10^3	2)	The decimal point moved 3 places, so the whole number in the power of ten is 3.
4.96×10^{-3}	3)	Since 0.00496 is less than 1, the power of ten must be negative.

You can convert a number from scientific notation to standard form in 3 steps.
1. Find the power of ten.
2. If the exponent is negative, you must move the decimal point to the left. Move it the number of places indicated by the whole number in the exponent.
3. Insert a leading zero before the decimal point.

Example
Write 1.23×10^{-5} in standard notation.

10^{-5}	1)	Find the power of ten.
.0000123	2)	The exponent is −5, so move the decimal point 5 places to the left.
0.0000123	3)	Insert a leading zero before the decimal point.

Write each number in scientific notation.

1. 0.0279

2. 0.00007100

3. 0.0000005060

Write each number in standard notation.

4. 2.350×10^{-4}

5. 6.5×10^{-3}

6. 7.07×10^{-5}

Name _____ Date _____ Class _____

LESSON 2-4 Operations with Scientific Notation
Practice and Problem Solving: A/B

Add or subtract. Write your answer in scientific notation.

1. $6.4 \times 10^3 + 1.4 \times 10^4 + 7.5 \times 10^3$ _____

2. $4.2 \times 10^6 - 1.2 \times 10^5 - 2.5 \times 10^5$ _____

3. $3.3 \times 10^9 + 2.6 \times 10^9 + 7.7 \times 10^8$ _____

4. $8.0 \times 10^4 - 3.4 \times 10^4 - 1.2 \times 10^3$ _____

Multiply or divide. Write your answer in scientific notation.

5. $(3.2 \times 10^8)(1.3 \times 10^9) = $ _____

6. $\dfrac{8.8 \times 10^7}{4.4 \times 10^4} = $ _____

7. $(1.5 \times 10^6)(5.9 \times 10^4) = $ _____

8. $\dfrac{1.44 \times 10^{10}}{2.4 \times 10^2} = $ _____

Write each number using calculator notation.

9. $4.1 \times 10^4 = $ _____

10. $9.4 \times 10^{-6} = $ _____

Write each number using scientific notation.

11. 5.2E–6 = _____

12. 8.3E+2 = _____

Use the situation below to complete Exercises 13–16. Express each answer in scientific notation.

A runner tries to keep a consistent stride length in a marathon. But, the length will change during the race. A runner has a stride length of 5 feet for the first half of the race and a stride length of 4.5 feet for the second half.

13. A marathon is 26 miles 385 yards long. That is about 1.4×10^5 feet. How many feet long is half a marathon?

    _____

14. How many strides would it take to finish the first half of the marathon?

    _____

Hint: Write 5 ft as 5.0×10^0 and 4.5 feet as 4.5×10^0.

15. How many strides would it take to finish the second half of the marathon?

    _____

16. How many strides would it take the runner to complete marathon? Express your answer in both scientific notation and standard notation.

    _____

Name _____ Date _____ Class _____

LESSON 2-4 Operations with Scientific Notation
Reteach

To add or subtract numbers written in scientific notation:

Check that the exponents of powers of 10 are the same.
If not, adjust the decimal numbers and the exponents.
Add or subtract the decimal numbers.
Write the sum or difference and the common power of 10 in scientific notation format.
Check whether the answer is in scientific notation.
If it is not, adjust the decimal and the exponent.

$(a \times 10^n) + (b \times 10^n) = (a + b) \times 10^n$ $(1.2 \times 10^5) - (9.5 \times 10^4)$
$(a \times 10^n) - (b \times 10^n) = (a - b) \times 10^n$ $(1.2 \times 10^5) - (0.95 \times 10^5)$ ← Adjust to get same
                                                                   $(1.2 - 0.95) \times 10^5$ exponent.
                                                                                0.25×10^5 ← Not in scientific notation.
                                                                                2.5×10^4 ← Answer

To multiply numbers written in scientific notation:

Multiply the decimal numbers.
Add the exponents in the powers of 10.
Check whether the answer is in scientific notation.
If it is not, adjust the decimal numbers and the exponent.

$(a \times 10^n) \times (b \times 10^m) = ab \times 10^{n+m}$ $(2.7 \times 10^8) \times (8.9 \times 10^4)$
                                                                                           $(2.7 \times 8.9) \times 10^{8+4}$
                                                                                                   24.03×10^{12} ← Not in scientific notation.
                                                                                                   2.403×10^{13} ← Answer

To divide numbers written in scientific notation:

Divide the decimal numbers.
Subtract the exponents in the powers of 10.
Check whether the answer is in scientific notation.
If it is not, adjust the decimal numbers and the exponent.

$(a \times 10^n) \div (b \times 10^m) = a \div b \times 10^{n-m}$ $(6.3 \times 10^7) \div (9.0 \times 10^3)$
                                                                                                 $(6.3 \div 9.0) \times 10^{7-3}$
                                                                                                     0.7×10^4 ← Not in scientific notation.
                                                                                                     7.0×10^3 ← Answer

Compute. Write each answer in scientific notation.

1. $(2.21 \times 10^7) \div (3.4 \times 10^4)$ 2. $(5.8 \times 10^6) - (4.3 \times 10^6)$ 3. $(2.8 \times 10^3)(7.5 \times 10^4)$

Name _____ Date _____ Class _____

LESSON 3-1 Representing Proportional Relationships
Practice and Problem Solving: A/B

Use the table to complete Exercises 1–3.

Feet	1		3	4		6
Inches		24			60	

1. The table shows the relationship between lengths in feet and lengths in inches. Complete the table.

2. Write each pair as a ratio. $\frac{\text{inches}}{\text{feet}} \to \frac{}{1} = \frac{24}{} = \frac{}{3} = \frac{}{4} = \frac{60}{} = \frac{}{6}$

   Each ratio is equal to _____.

3. Let x represent feet. Let y represent inches.

   An equation that describes the relationship is _____.

Use the table to complete Exercises 4 and 5. Tell whether each relationship is proportional. If it is proportional, write an equation that describes the relationship. First define your variables.

Lemonade Recipe

Lemons	1	2	3	4	5	6
Sugar (c)	1.5	3	4.5	6	7.5	9
Water (c)	7	14	21	28	35	42

4. the ratio of lemons to cups of sugar

   _____

5. the ratio of cups of sugar to cups of water

   _____

Use the table to complete Exercise 6.

Distance Traveled Daily on a Family Road Trip

Hours	6	4.5	9	2	3.25	5.75
Distance (mi)	270	229.5	495	60	188.5	281.75

6. Is the relationship shown in the table below proportional? If so, what is the ratio of the hours driven to miles traveled?

   _____

Name _____ Date _____ Class _____

LESSON 3-1
Representing Proportional Relationships
Reteach

A **proportional relationship** is a relationship between two sets of quantities in which the ratio of one quantity to the other quantity is constant. If you divide any number in one group by the corresponding number in the other group, you will always get the same quotient.

Example: Martin mixes a cleaning spray that is 1 part vinegar to 5 parts water.

Proportional relationships can be shown in tables, graphs, or equations.

Table

The table below shows the number of cups of vinegar Martin needs to add to certain amounts of water to mix his cleaning spray.

Martin's Cleaning Spray

Water (c)	5	10	15	20	25
Vinegar (c)	1	2	3	4	5

Notice that if you divide the amount of water by the amount of vinegar, the quotient is always 5.

Graph

On the graph, you can see that for every 1 unit you move to the right on the *x*-axis, you move up 5 units on the *y*-axis.

Equation

Let *y* represent the number of cups of water.
Let *x* represent the cups of vinegar.

$y = 5x$

Use the table below for Exercises 1–3.

Distance driven (mi)	100	200		400		600
Gas used (gal)	5		15			30

1. There is a proportional relationship between the distance a car drives and the amount of gas used. Complete the table.

2. Find each ratio. $\dfrac{\text{miles}}{\text{gallons}} \rightarrow \dfrac{100}{5} = \dfrac{200}{} = \dfrac{}{15} = \dfrac{400}{} = \dfrac{}{} = \dfrac{600}{30}$

   Each ratio is equal to _____.

3. a. Let *x* represent gallons of gas used. Let *y* represent _____.

   b. The equation that describes the relationship is _____.

Name _____ Date _____ Class _____

LESSON 3-2
Rate of Change and Slope
Practice and Problem Solving: A/B

Find the slope of each line.

1. slope = _____

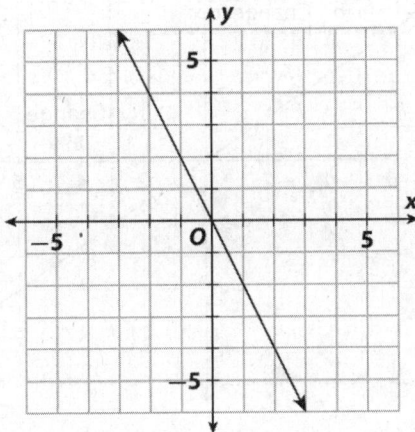

2. slope = _____

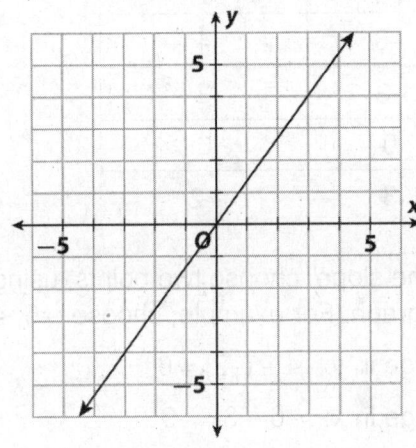

Solve.

3. Jasmine bought 7 yards of fabric. The total cost was $45.43. What was the average cost per yard of the fabric she bought?

    _____

4. A train traveled 325 miles in 5 hours. What was the train's average rate of speed in miles per hour?

    _____

5. The graph at the right shows the amount of water in a tank that is being filled. What is the average rate of change in gallons per minute?

    _____

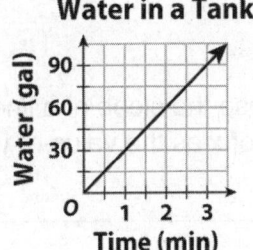

6. Suppose the size of the tank in question 5 is doubled. Will the average rate of change in gallons per minute change? Explain your answer.

    _____

    _____

7. A line passes through (1, 1), (−2, 4), and (6, n). Find the value of n.

    _____

LESSON 3-2: Rate of Change and Slope
Reteach

Look at the relationships between the table, the graph, and the slope.

First value (x)	Second value (y)
−6	4
−3	2
0	0
3	−2

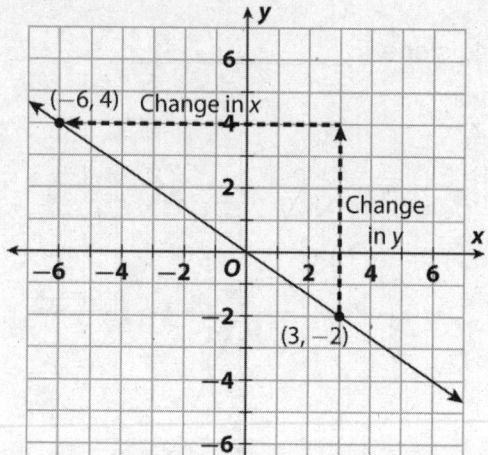

To find the slope, choose two points, using the table or graph. For example, choose (−6, 4) and (3, −2).

Change in y: $4 - (-2) = 6$

Change in x: $-6 - 3 = -9$

Slope = $\dfrac{\text{change in } y}{\text{change in } x} = \dfrac{6}{-9} = -\dfrac{2}{3}$

Use the example above to complete Exercises 1 and 2.

1. The slope is negative. In the table, as the values of x decrease, the values of y _____.

2. The slope is negative. In the graph, as you move from left to right, the line of the graph is going _____ (up or down).

Solve.

3. Suppose the slope of a line is positive. Describe what happens to the value of x as the value of y increases.

   _____

   _____

4. Suppose the slope of a line is positive. Describe what happens to the graph of the line as you move from left to right.

   _____

   _____

5. Two points on a line are (3, 8) and (−3, 2). What is the slope of the line?

   _____

Name _____ Date _____ Class _____

LESSON 3-3 Interpreting the Unit Rate as Slope
Practice and Problem Solving: A/B

Find the slope. Name the unit rate.

1. **Benjamin Hiking**

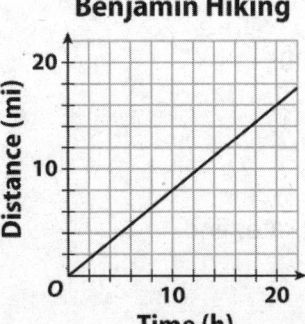

Slope = _____

Unit rate: _____

2. **Marcy Hiking**

Time (h)	5	10	15	20
Distance (mi)	6	12	18	24

Slope = _____

Unit rate: _____

3. The equation $y = 3.5x$ represents the rate, in miles per hour, at which Laura walks.

   The graph at right represents the rate at which Piyush walks. Determine who walks faster. Explain.

   _____

   _____

   Piyush Walking

4. Rain fell at a steady rate of 2 inches every 3 hours.

   a. Complete the table to describe the relationship.

Time (h)	3		12
Rainfall (in.)		4	6

   b. Graph the data in the table on the coordinate grid at right. Draw the line.

   c. Find the slope.

   _____

   d. Identify the unit rate.

   _____

   Rainfall

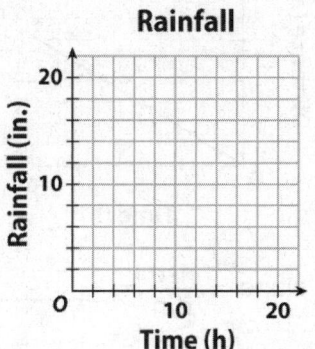

Original content Copyright © by Houghton Mifflin Harcourt. Additions and changes to the original content are the responsibility of the instructor.

Name _____ Date _____ Class _____

LESSON 3-3 Interpreting the Unit Rate as Slope
Reteach

A **rate** is a comparison of two quantities that have different units.

A **unit rate** is a rate in which the second quantity is 1 unit.

For example, walking 10 miles every *5 hours* is a rate. Walking 2 miles every *1 hour* is the equivalent unit rate.

$$\frac{10 \text{ miles}}{5 \text{ hours}} = \frac{2 \text{ miles}}{1 \text{ hour}} = 2 \text{ mi/h}$$

The slope of a graph represents the unit rate. To find the unit rate, find the slope.

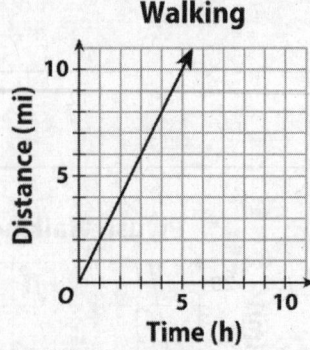

Step 1: Use the origin and another point to find the slope.

$$\text{slope} = \frac{\text{rise}}{\text{run}} = \frac{10 - 0}{5 - 0} = \frac{10}{5} = 2$$

Step 2: Write the slope as the unit rate.

slope = unit rate = 2 mi/h

Find the slope of the graph and the unit rate.

1. **Scott Hiking**

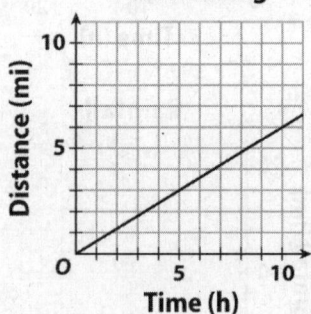

slope = $\frac{\text{rise}}{\text{run}}$ = _____

unit rate = _____ mi/h

2. **Rebecca Hiking**

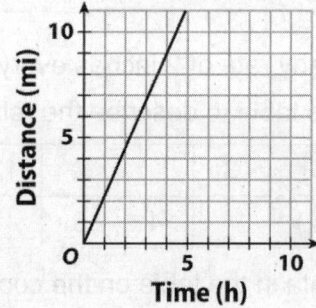

slope = $\frac{\text{rise}}{\text{run}}$ = _____

unit rate = _____ mi/h

LESSON 4-1 Representing Linear Nonproportional Relationships
Practice and Problem Solving: A/B

Make a table of values for each equation.

1. $y = 4x + 3$

x	−2	−1	0	1	2
y					

2. $y = \frac{1}{4}x - 2$

x	−8	−4	0	4	8
y					

3. $y = -0.5x + 1$

x	−4	−2	0	2	4
y					

4. $y = 3x + 5$

x	−2	−1	0	1	2
y					

Make a table of values and graph the solutions of each equation.

5. $y = 2x + 1$

x	−2	−1	0	1	2
y					

6. $y = -\frac{1}{2}x - 3$

x	−4	−2	0	2	4
y					

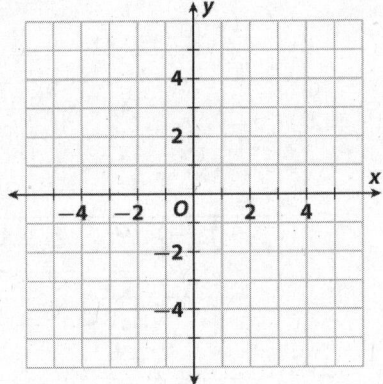
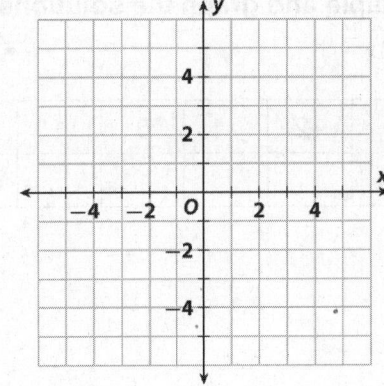

State whether the graph of each linear relationship is a solid line or a set of unconnected points. Explain your reasoning.

7. The relationship between the height of a tree and the time since the tree was planted.

_____

_____

8. The relationship between the number of $12 DVDs you buy and the total cost.

_____

Name _____ Date _____ Class _____

LESSON 4-1
Representing Linear Nonproportional Relationships
Reteach

A relationship will be proportional if the ratios in a table of values of the relationship are constant. The graph of a proportional relationship will be a straight line through the origin. If either of these is not true, the relationship is nonproportional.

To graph the solutions of an equation, make a table of values. Choose values that will give integer solutions.

A. Graph the solutions of $y = x + 2$.

x	−2	−1	0	1	2
y	0	1	2	3	4

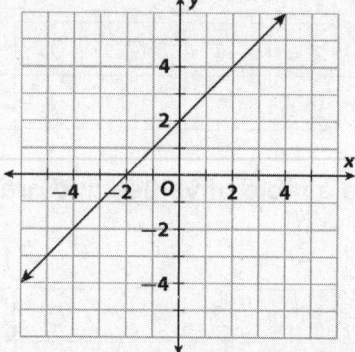

B. Tell whether the relationship is proportional. Explain.

The graph is a straight line, but it does **not** go through the origin, so the relationship is not proportional.

Make a table and graph the solutions of each equation.

1. $y = 3x + 1$

x	−2	−1	0	1	2
y					

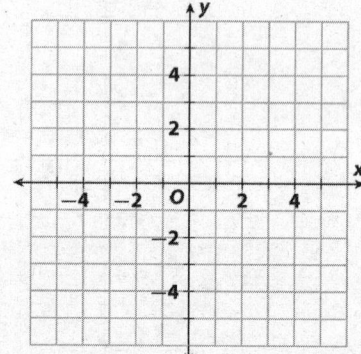

2. $y = -x - 2$

x	−2	−1	0	1	2
y					

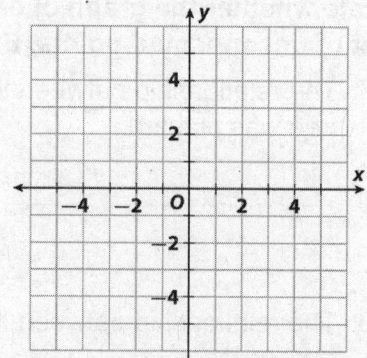

Name _____ Date _____ Class _____

LESSON 4-2 Determining Slope and y-intercept
Practice and Problem Solving: A/B

Find the slope and y-intercept of the line in each graph.

1.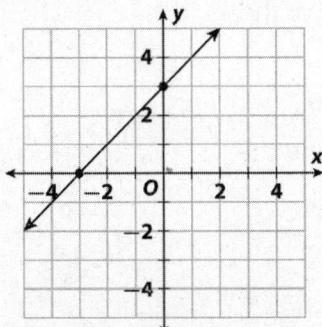

   slope $m =$ _____

   y-intercept $b =$ _____

2.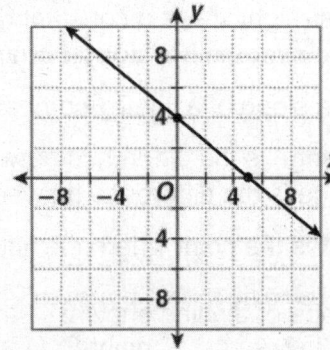

   slope $m =$ _____

   y-intercept $b =$ _____

Find the slope and y-intercept of the line represented by each table.

3.
x	0	3	6	9	12
y		10	19	28	37

slope $m =$ _____

y-intercept $b =$ _____

4.
x	0	2	4	6	8
y		2	3	4	5

slope $m =$ _____

y-intercept $b =$ _____

Find and interpret the rate of change and the initial value.

5. A pizzeria charges $8 for a large cheese pizza, plus $2 for each topping. The total cost for a large pizza is given by the equation $C = 2t + 8$, where t is the number of toppings. Graph the equation for t between 0 and 5 toppings, and explain the meaning of the slope and y-intercept.

   _____

   _____

   _____

LESSON 4-2 Determining Slope and y-intercept
Reteach

The **slope** of a line is a measure of its tilt, or slant.

The slope of a straight line is a constant ratio, the "rise over run," or the **vertical change** over the **horizontal change.**

You can find the slope of a line by comparing any two of its points.

The vertical change is the difference between the two y-values, and the horizontal change is the difference between the two x-values.

The **y-intercept** is the point where the line crosses the y-axis.

A. Find the slope of the line shown.
   point A: (3, 2)   point B: (4, 4)

   $$\text{slope} = \frac{4-2}{4-3}$$
   $$= \frac{2}{1}, \text{ or } 2$$

   So, the slope of the line is 2.

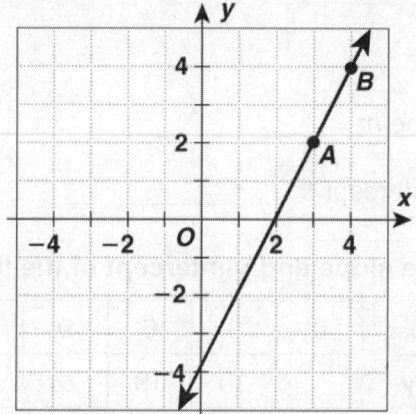

B. Find the y-intercept of the line shown.
   The line crosses the y-axis at (0, –4).
   So, the y-intercept is –4.

Find the slope and y-intercept of the line in each graph.

1.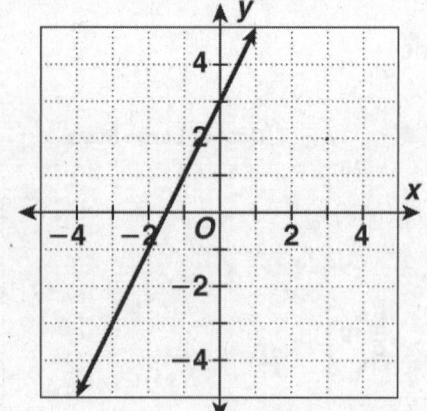

2.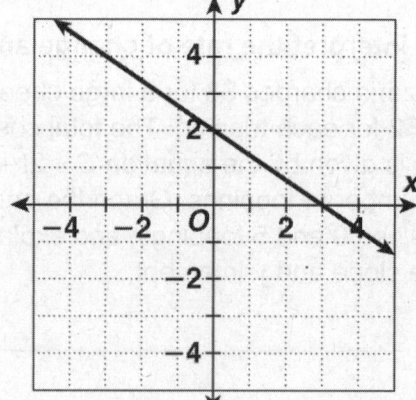

slope m = _____   slope m = _____

y-intercept b = _____   y-intercept b = _____

Name _____ Date _____ Class _____

LESSON 4-3
Graphing Linear Nonproportional Relationships Using Slope and *y*-intercept

Practice and Problem Solving: A/B

Graph each equation using the slope and the *y*-intercept.

1. $y = 2x - 1$

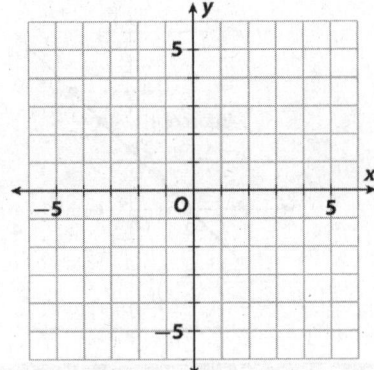

slope = _____ *y*-intercept = _____

2. $y = \dfrac{1}{2}x + 3$

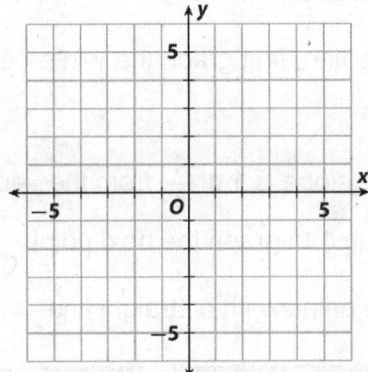

slope = _____ *y*-intercept = _____

3. $y = x - 4$

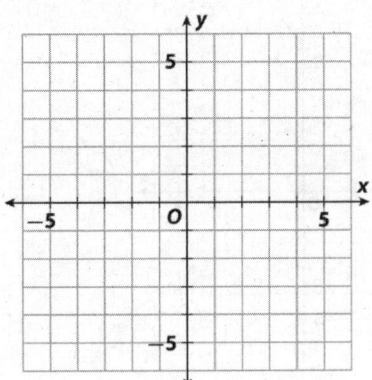

slope = _____ *y*-intercept = _____

4. $y = -x - 2$

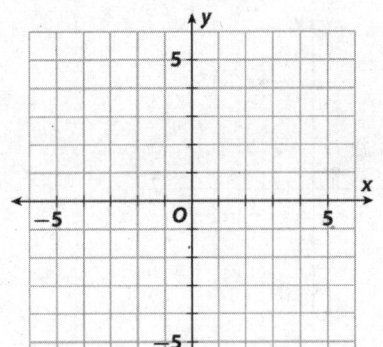

slope = _____ *y*-intercept = _____

5. The equation $y = 15x + 10$ gives your score on a math quiz, where *x* is the number of questions you answered correctly.

   a. Graph the equation.

   b. Interpret the slope and *y*-intercept of the line.

   _____

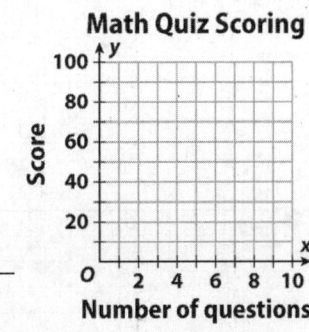

   c. What is your score if you answered 5 questions correctly?

   _____

LESSON 4-3

Graphing Linear Nonproportional Relationships Using Slope and *y*-intercept

Reteach

You can graph a linear function by graphing the *y*-intercept of the line and then using the slope to find other points on the line.

The graph shows $y = x + 2$.

To graph the line, first graph the *y*-intercept which is located at (0, 2).

Because the slope is 1 or $\frac{1}{1}$, from the *y*-intercept, rise 1 and run 1 to graph the next point.

Connect the points with a straight line.

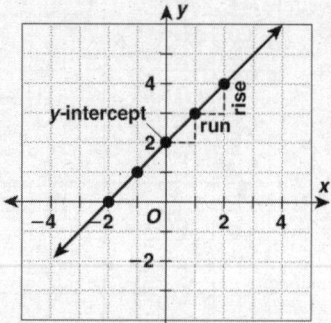

Graph each equation using the slope and the *y*-intercept.

1. $y = 4x - 1$

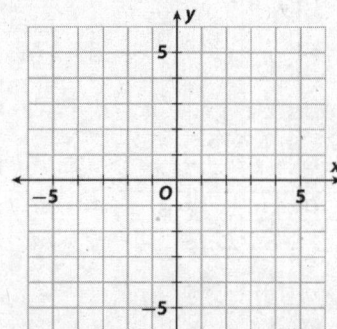

slope = _____ *y*-intercept = _____

2. $y = -\frac{1}{2}x + 2$

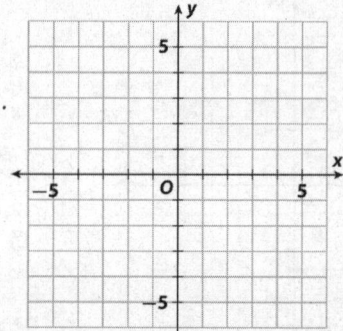

slope = _____ *y*-intercept = _____

3. $y = -x + 1$

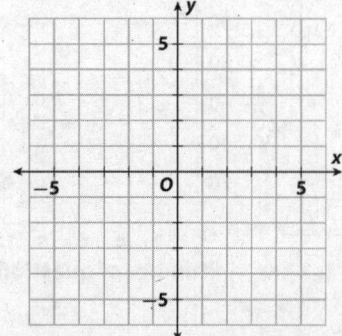

slope = _____ *y*-intercept = _____

4. $y = 2x - 3$

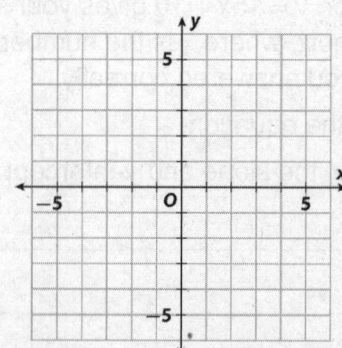

slope = _____ *y*-intercept = _____

LESSON 4-4 Proportional and Nonproportional Situations
Practice and Problem Solving: A/B

Determine if each relationship is a proportional or nonproportional situation. Explain your reasoning. (Assume that the tables represent linear relationships.)

1.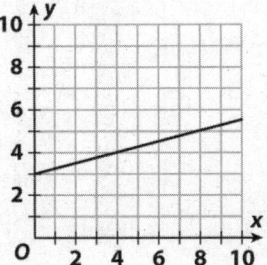

_____
_____

2.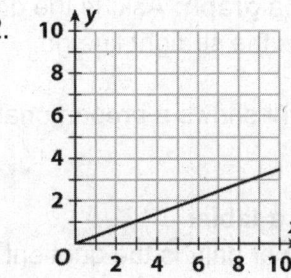

_____
_____

3. $t = 15d$

_____
_____

4. $m = 0.75d - 2$

_____
_____

5. $y = \sqrt{x}$

_____
_____

6. $r = b^2 + 1$

_____
_____

7.
x	y
2	11
5	26
12	61

_____
_____

8.
x	y
4	36
10	90
13	117

_____
_____

LESSON 4-4: Proportional and Nonproportional Situations
Reteach

To decide whether a relationship is proportional or nonproportional, consider how the relationship is presented.

If the relationship is a **graph**: Ask: Is the graph a straight line? Does the straight line go through the origin?
The graph at the right shows a proportional relationship.

If the relationship is a **table**:
Ask: For every number pair, is the quotient of y and x constant? Will (0, 0) fit the pattern?
The table at the right shows a proportional relationship. The quotient for every number pair is 5. Since each y-value is 5 times each x-value, (0, 0) will fit the pattern.

x	y
4	20
6	30
7	35

If the relationship is an **equation**:
Ask: Is the equation linear? When the equation is written in the form $y = mx + b$ is the value of b equal to 0?
The equation at the right shows a proportional relationship.

$y = 0.8x$

Determine if each relationship is a proportional or non-proportional situation. Explain your reasoning.

1.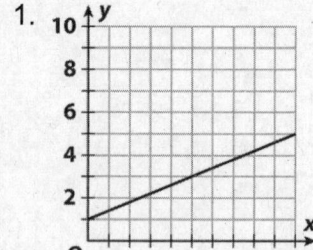

2.
x	y
3	36
5	60
8	96

_____

_____

3. $y = x^3$

_____

_____

4. $q = 4b$

_____

_____

Name _____ Date _____ Class _____

LESSON 5-1
Writing Linear Equations from Situations and Graphs
Practice and Problem Solving: A/B

For each situation described in Exercises 1–4, first write an equation in the form $y = mx + b$. Then, solve each problem.

1. A sales associate is given a $500 hiring bonus with a new job. She earns an average commission of $250 per week for the next 12 weeks. How much does she earn?

   _____
   _____

2. A farm has 75 acres of wheat. The farmer can harvest the wheat from 12 acres per day. In how many days will all of the fields be harvested?

   _____
   _____

3. A contractor's crew can frame 3 houses in a week. How long will it take them to frame 54 houses if they frame the same number each week?

   _____
   _____

4. A water tank holds 18,000 gallons. How long will it take for the water level to reach 6000 gallons if the water is used at an average rate of 450 gallons per day?

   _____
   _____

Write an equation in the form $y = mx + b$ for each situation.

5.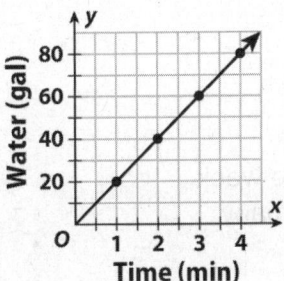

6.
Height (m)y	Time (s)x
360	0
300	10
240	20
180	30
120	40

_____   _____

Name _____ Date _____ Class _____

Writing Linear Equations from Situations and Graphs
LESSON 5-1
Reteach

You will be asked to find the slope (*m*) and the *y*-intercept (*b*) of graphs of linear equations in the form $y = mx + b$. Both slope and *y*-intercept can be identified from the wording of a problem.

y-intercept, b

- No initial or beginning value means $b = 0$.
- A nonzero beginning or starting means $b \neq 0$.

slope, m

- A rate indicates slope, *m*.
- A change "per" some variable;
  - increasing ($m > 0$)
  - decreasing ($m < 0$)

Example

The concession stand has 500 pom-poms before the game. The fans bought them at a rate of 25 per minute. How long will it take for the supply to be gone?

What is *b*? ⟶ $b = 500$

What is *m* and why is it negative? ⟶ $m = -25$, because 25 are being sold each minute.

What else do you know? ⟶ In the equation, $y = 0$ when all of the pom-poms are sold.

Replace the variables in the equation: $y = mx + b$ ⟶ $0 = -25t + 500$

$25t = 500$

Solve for *t* $t = 20$ minutes

Write the slope, *y*-intercept, and equation for each situation.

1. The race begins at a rate of 1.5 meters per second. What distance, *d*, is covered after *t* seconds?

   Slope _____; *y*-intercept: _____

   Equation: _____

2. Fifty azalea plants arrive at a florist's shop on the first day of the week. After that, they arrive at an average of 75 plants per day. How many plants will be at the shop after *t* days?

   Slope: _____; *y*-intercept: _____

   Equation: _____

Original content Copyright © by Houghton Mifflin Harcourt. Additions and changes to the original content are the responsibility of the instructor.

Name _____ Date _____ Class _____

LESSON 5-2 Writing Linear Equations from a Table
Practice and Problem Solving: A/B

Graph the data, and find the slope and y-intercept from the graph. Then write an equation for the graph in slope-intercept form.

1.

Weight (oz), x	2	4	8	10
Cost ($), y	12	16	24	28

2.

Time (min), x	5	20	30	35
Elevation (ft), y	4	10	14	16

slope: _____

y-intercept: _____

equation: _____

slope: _____

y-intercept: _____

equation: _____

Write an equation in slope-intercept form that represents the data.

3.

Sales Per Day, x	0	1	2	3
Daily Pay ($), y	100	105	110	115

equation: _____

4.

Time Since Turning Oven Off (min), x	0	5	10	15
Temperature of Oven (°F), y	375	325	275	225

equation: _____

The table shows the linear relationship of the height y (in inches) of a tomato plant x weeks after it was planted.

Weeks After Planting, x	Height (in.), y
0	8
1	11
2	14
3	17

5. Write an equation that shows the height of the tomato plant.

_____

6. Use the equation to find the height of the tomato plant 6 weeks after it was planted.

_____

Original content Copyright © by Houghton Mifflin Harcourt. Additions and changes to the original content are the responsibility of the instructor.

LESSON 5-2 Writing Linear Equations from a Table
Reteach

A linear relationship can be described using an equation in slope-intercept form, $y = mx + b$, where m is the slope and b is the y-intercept. Recall that the y-intercept b is where the graph of the equation crosses the y-axis, which is at point $(0, b)$.

The table below shows the linear relationship between the hours is takes to repair a car and the total cost of the repairs, including the cost of the parts.

Look for an x-value of 0. The corresponding y-value, 325, is the y-intercept.

Hours Worked, x	Total Cost ($), y
0	325
2	425
4	525
6	625

+2   +100

Find changes in x-values and y-values. Then use the values to find the slope:

$$m = \frac{\text{change in } y\text{-values}}{\text{change in } x\text{-values}} = \frac{100}{2} = 50$$

Using x-values that differ by 1 will require the least calculation.

Use the y-intercept, $b = 325$, and the slope, $m = 50$ to write an equation for the relationship.
$y = mx + b$
$y = 50x + 325$

Write an equation in slope-intercept form for each linear relationship.

1. The total monthly cost, y, for smartphone service depends on the number of text messages, x.

Text Messages, x	0	10	20	30
Cost ($), y	40.00	42.00	44.00	46.00

slope: _____
y-intercept: _____
equation: _____

2. The total cost, y, for a taxi ride depends on the number of miles traveled, x.

Distance (mi), x	0	1	5	10
Total Cost ($), y	2.50	5.00	15.00	27.50

slope: _____
y-intercept: _____
equation: _____

Lesson 5-3 Linear Relationships and Bivariate Data
Practice and Problem Solving: A/B

Does each of the tables represent a linear relationship? Explain why or why not.

1.
Months	0	1	2
Account balance ($)	220	240	260

_____

2.
Time (sec)	2	3	4
Distance (ft)	8	12	15

_____

Write an equation for each linear relationship.

3.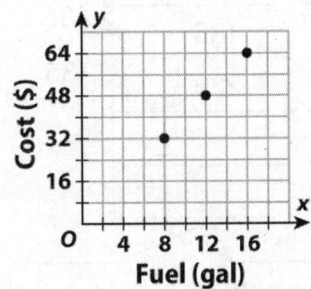

_____

4.
Weight (lb), x	Total cost ($), y
1	10
2	12
4	16
6	20

_____

The graph shows the relationship between the number of rows in a friendship bracelet and the time it takes Mia to make the bracelet, including the time it takes to prepare the threads.

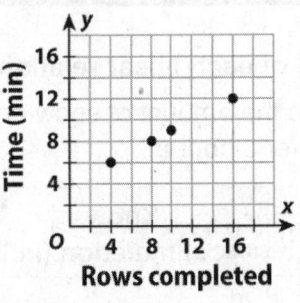

5. Determine whether the relationship is linear. If so, write an equation for the relationship.

_____

6. How long will it take for Mia to complete 14 rows?

_____

7. Mia teaches Brynn how to make a bracelet. Graph these points to show Brynn's progress: (2, 6), (4, 8), (8, 10), (12, 12). Is the time y it takes Brynn to make a bracelet with x rows a linear relationship? Explain.

_____

Name _____ Date _____ Class _____

LESSON 5-3 Linear Relationships and Bivariate Data
Reteach

You have used an equation of a linear relationship to predict a value between two data points that you know. You can also use a table of a linear relationship to predict a value.

The table below shows the linear relationship between the number of months a company hosts a website and the total cost of hosting the website, including the set-up fee. What is the cost for 4 months of web hosting?

Months	Total Cost ($)
2	125
6	265
8	335

+2 ↓ +70

Find rate of change.
An increase of 2 months increases the cost by $70. So, the monthly cost increase is:

$$\frac{\text{change in cost}}{\text{change in months}} = \frac{70}{2} = 35$$

Months	Total Cost ($)
2	125
3	160
4	195
5	230
6	265
8	335

+35, +35, +35

Fill in missing values.
Use the rate of change, 35, to fill in the numbers between the given numbers. Start at month 2.

Looking at the second table, the cost for 4 months of web hosting is $195.

Use the table of each linear relationship to find each value.

1. Determine the amount of snow on the ground after 3 hours.

Time (h)	Snow Accumulation (in.)
1	5
4	11
5	13

2. Determine the total cost of 6 prints of a digital photo.

Prints	Total Cost ($)
2	3.00
4	6.00
7	10.50

Original content Copyright © by Houghton Mifflin Harcourt. Additions and changes to the original content are the responsibility of the instructor.

Name _____ Date _____ Class _____

LESSON 6-1
Identifying and Representing Functions
Practice and Problem Solving: A/B

Tell whether each relationship is a function.

1.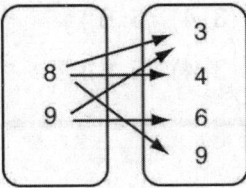

2.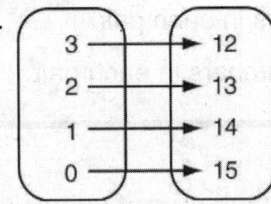

3.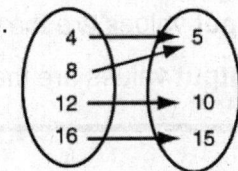

_____

_____

_____

4.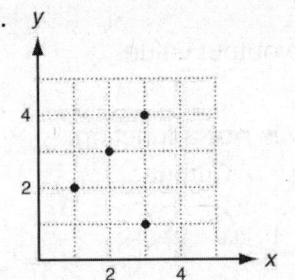

5.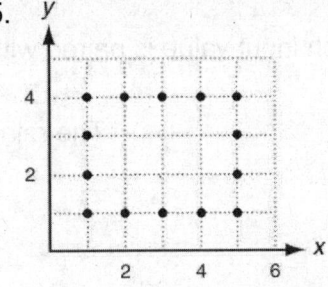

6.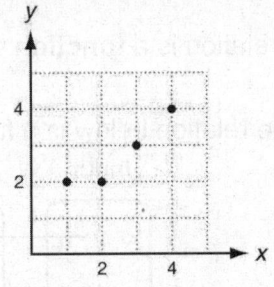

_____

_____

_____

7.
Input	0	1	2	3
Output	4	1	0	4

8.
Input	1	2	0	1	2
Output	4	5	6	7	8

_____

_____

9. {(0, 0), (2, 4), (3, 6), (5, 5), (7, 6)}

10. {(0, 8), (1, 2), (3, 7), (5, 9), (3, 6)}

_____

_____

The graph shows the relationship between the hours Rachel studied and the exam grades she earned.

11. Is the relationship a function? Justify your answer. Use the words "input" and "output" in your explanation, and connect them to the context represented by the graph.

   _____

   _____

12. Rachel plans to study 2 hours for her next exam. How might plotting her grade on the same graph change your answer to Exercise 11? Explain your reasoning.

   _____

   _____

Original content Copyright © by Houghton Mifflin Harcourt. Additions and changes to the original content are the responsibility of the instructor.

LESSON 6-1
Identifying and Representing Functions
Reteach

A **relation** is a set of ordered pairs.   {(1, 2), (3, 4), (5, 6)}

The **input** values are the first numbers in each pair.   {(**1**, 2), (**3**, 4), (**5**, 6)}

The **output** values are the second numbers in each pair.   {(1, **2**), (3, **4**), (5, **6**)}

Circle each input value. Underline each output value.

1. {(1, 1), (2, 3), (3, 5)}
2. {(6, 2), (5, 3), (4, 8)}

A relation is a **function** when each input value is paired with *only one* output value.

The relation below is a function.

Input value 2 is paired with *only one* output, 5.
Input value 1 is paired with *only one* output, 1.
Input value 3 is paired with *only one* output, 1.

The relation below is **not** a function.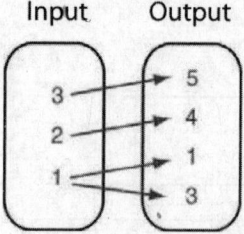

Input value 1 is paired with *two* outputs, 1 and 3.

Tell whether each relation is a function. Explain how you know.

3. {(1, 5), (3, 7), (6, 5), (9, 8)}

_____

4. {(1, 2), (1, 8), (3, 6), (4, 8)}

_____

5.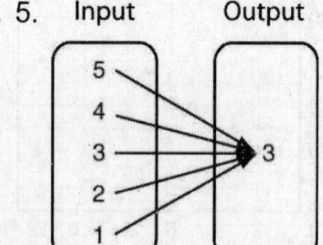

_____

_____

6.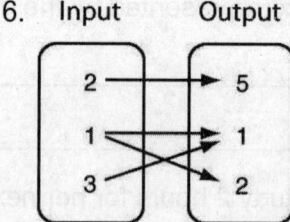

_____

_____

Name _____ Date _____ Class _____

LESSON 6-2 Describing Functions
Practice and Problem Solving: A/B

Graph each equation. Tell whether the equation is linear or nonlinear.

1. $y = 3x$

Input, x	−1	0	1	2	4
Output, y					

2. $y = x^2 + 1$

Input, x	−2	−1	0	1	2
Output, y					

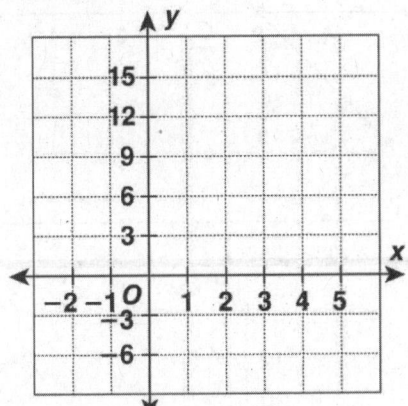
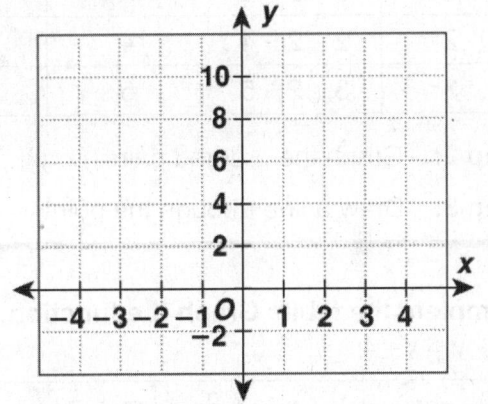

_____   _____

Tell whether each equation can be written in the form $y = mx + b$. Write yes or no. If yes, write the equation in the form $y = mx + b$.

3. $y = 8 - x^2$ 4. $y = 4 + x$ 5. $y = 3 - 2x$

_____   _____   _____

The amount of water in a tank being filled is represented by the equation $y = 20x$, where y is the number of gallons in the tank after x minutes.

6. Complete the table of values for this situation.

Time (min), x	0	1	2		4
Water (gal), y				60	

7. Sketch a graph of the equation.

8. Use your graph to predict the amount of water in the tank after 6 minutes.

_____

9. Explain how you know whether relationship between x and y is linear or nonlinear.

_____

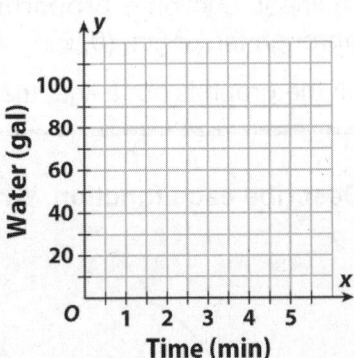

Name _____ Date _____ Class _____

LESSON 6-2 Describing Functions
Reteach

Graph $y = x + 2$.

Step 1: Make a table of values.

Input, x	x + 2	Output, y	(x, y)
−2	−2 + 2 = 0	0	(−2, 0)
0	0 + 2 = 2	2	(0, 2)
2	2 + 2 = 4	4	(2, 4)
3	3 + 2 = 5	5	(3, 5)

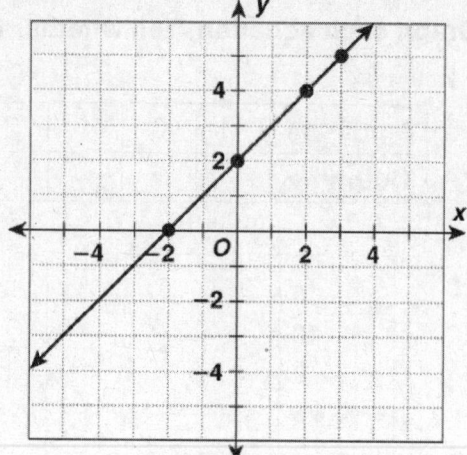

Step 2: Graph the ordered pairs, (x, y).
Step 3: Draw a line through the points.

Complete the table. Graph the function.

1. $y = x + 4$

Input, x	x + 4	Output, y	(x, y)
−2	−2 + 4 = ___		(−2, ___)
0	___ + 4 = ___		
2			
6			
8			

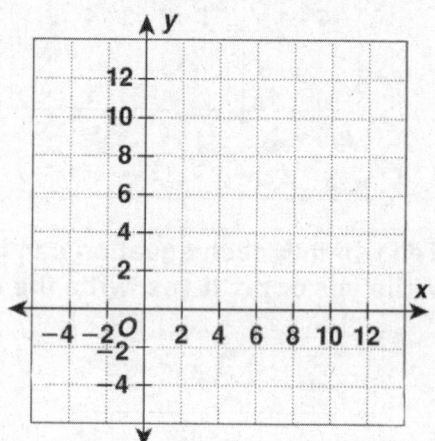

A function is **linear** if:
- the graph is a line, and
- the equation can be written in the form $y = mx + b$.

A linear function is **proportional** if its graph passes through the origin, (0, 0).

If the graph is not a line, then the function is **nonlinear**.

Linear: $y = mx + b$
$y = 4 − 3x$ ⟶ $y = −3x + 4$
$y = 5x$ ⟶ $y = 5x + 0$

Proportional: $y = 5x$
                 $0 = 5(0)$

Not proportional: $y = 4 − 3x$
                     $0 \neq 4 − 3(0)$

Describe each function. Write *linear*, *proportional*, or *nonlinear*.

2.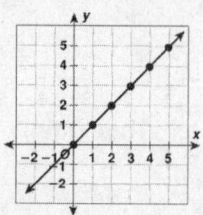

3. $y = −2x + 5$

4.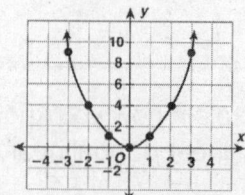

Name _____ Date _____ Class _____

LESSON 6-3 Comparing Functions
Practice and Problem Solving: A/B

Find the slopes of linear functions f and g. Then compare the slopes.

1. $f(x) = 5x - 2$

x	0	1	2	3	4
g(x)	-3	-1	1	3	5

slope of f = _____   slope of g = _____

_____

Find the y-intercepts of linear functions f and g. Then compare the two intercepts.

2.
x	0	1	2	3	4
f(x)	-3	-1	1	3	5

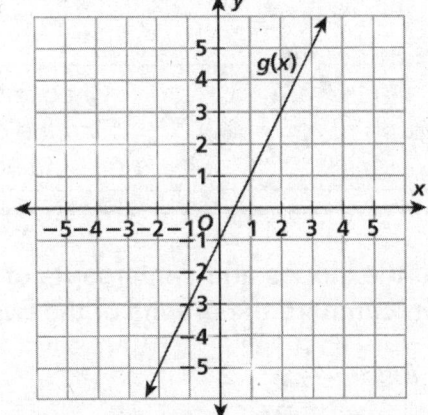

y-intercept of f: _____

y-intercept of g: _____

_____
_____

Connor and Pilar are in a rock-climbing club. They are climbing down a canyon wall. Connor starts from a cliff that is 200 feet above the canyon floor and climbs down at an average speed of 10 feet per minute. Pilar climbs down the canyon wall as shown in the table.

Time (min)	0	1	2	3
Pilar's height (ft)	242	234	226	218

3. Interpret the rates of change and initial values of the linear functions in terms of the situations that they model. Compare the results and what they mean.

Connor   Pilar

Initial value: _____   Initial value: _____

Rate of change: _____   Rate of change: _____

_____
_____

Original content Copyright © by Houghton Mifflin Harcourt. Additions and changes to the original content are the responsibility of the instructor.

Name _____ Date _____ Class _____

LESSON 6-3 Comparing Functions
Reteach

Functions can be represented in many forms. You can identify the slope and *y*-intercept from any format.

Representation	Slope	y-intercept
Equation written in slope-intercept form: $y = mx + b$	Value of *m*	Value of *b*
Table of values	Substitute any two ordered pairs into the slope formula. $m = \dfrac{y_2 - y_1}{x_2 - x_1}$	Substitute the slope and one ordered pair (*x*, *y*) into the slope-intercept formula. $y = mx + b$ Solve for *b*.
Graph	Choose two points on the line. Find the ratio of vertical change to horizontal change.	Find the point where the line crosses the *y*-axis. You may need to extend the graph.

Find the slopes and *y*-intercepts of the linear functions *f* and *g*. Then compare the graphs of the two functions.

1. $f(x) = -\dfrac{1}{2}x - 2$

x	−2	0	2	4	6
g(x)	4	1	−2	−5	−8

slope of *f* = _____   slope of *g* = _____

y-intercept of *f*: _____   *y*-intercept of *g*: _____

_____

_____

2. $f(x) = 6x - 1$

slope: of *f* = _____   of *g* = _____

y-intercept: of *f* = _____   of *g* = _____

_____

_____

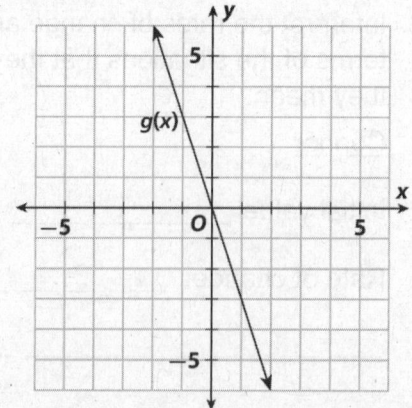

Original content Copyright © by Houghton Mifflin Harcourt. Additions and changes to the original content are the responsibility of the instructor.

Name _____ Date _____ Class _____

LESSON 6-4 Analyzing Graphs
Practice and Problem Solving: A/B

Use the situation for 1–2.

Dan is going to fix dinner. He turns on the oven. The graph shows the temperature over time.

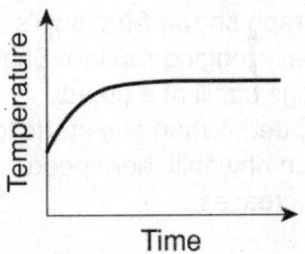

1. Why does the graph not start at zero?

   _____

   _____

2. What does it mean when the graph flattens out?

   _____

Tell which graph corresponds to each situation below.

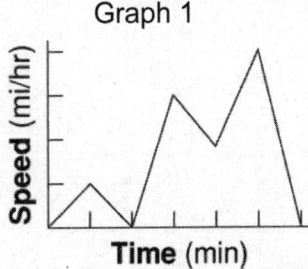
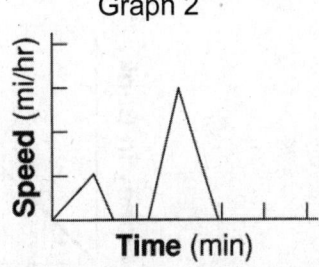
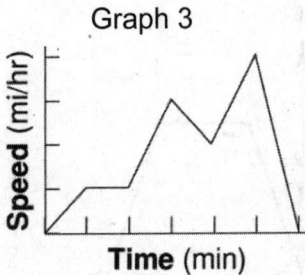

3. A car eases into traffic and then slows down and stops at an intersection. Next it enters the highway and adjusts speed to traffic until it exits and stops at home.   _____

4. A car eases into traffic, maintains speed for a short time. Next it enters the highway and adjusts speed to traffic until it exits and stops at home.   _____

5. Which graph did you not choose for Exercise 3 or Exercise 4? Write a description that describes what happened in that graph.

   _____

   _____

Use the graph at the right for 6–7.

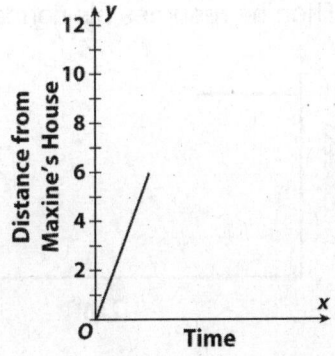

6. Maxine bikes 6 miles from home. She then rests for a short time before biking 4 more miles. After a short rest, she bikes home. Complete the graph so it shows the distance Maxine is from home compared to the time.

7. Find the total number of miles Maxine biked.

   _____

Name _____ Date _____ Class _____

LESSON 6-4 Analyzing Graphs
Reteach

Graphs are often used to model situations. This graph shows Shavawn's daily jogging routine. She jogs uphill at a steady speed. When she starts to run downhill, her speed increases.

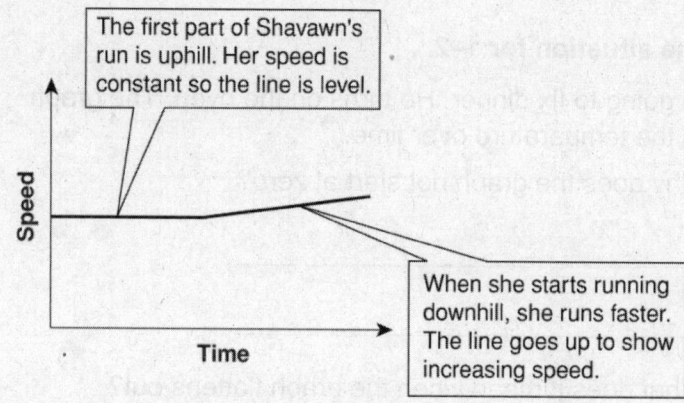

The first part of Shavawn's run is uphill. Her speed is constant so the line is level.

When she starts running downhill, she runs faster. The line goes up to show increasing speed.

You have a savings account in a bank. The graphs below show how the amount in your account changes. Describe what each graph shows.

1.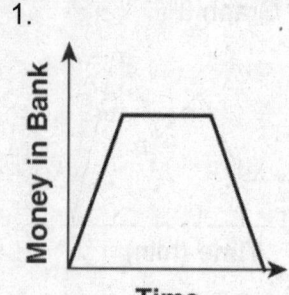

_____
_____
_____

2.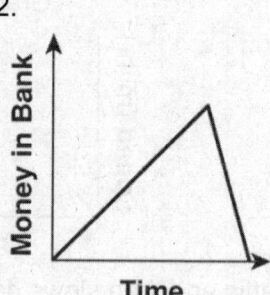

_____
_____
_____

Complete the graph for each situation.

3. Mr. Wyatt drives for a while at a steady speed. A traffic jam slows him down. Then he resumes his normal speed.

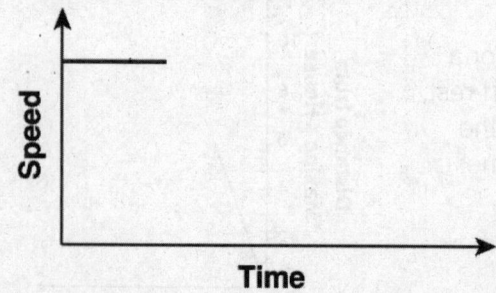

4. You are watching television. You turn down the volume during a commercial. You turn the volume back up after the commercial.

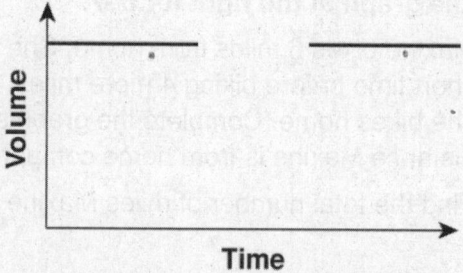

Original content Copyright © by Houghton Mifflin Harcourt. Additions and changes to the original content are the responsibility of the instructor.

Name _____ Date _____ Class _____

LESSON 7-1 Equations with the Variable on Both Sides
Practice and Problem Solving: A/B

Use algebra tiles to model and solve each equation.

1. $x + 3 = -x - 5$
2. $1 - 2x = -x - 3$
3. $x - 2 = -3x + 2$

_____ _____ _____

Fill in the boxes to solve each equation.

4. $\quad 4a - 3 = 2a + 7$
    $\quad -2a \qquad -[\ ]$
    $\overline{\quad 2a - 3 = 7}$
    $\quad +[\ ] \quad +3$
    $\overline{\qquad 2a = [\ ]}$
    $\quad \dfrac{2a}{[\ ]} = \dfrac{10}{[\ ]}$
    $\qquad a = [\ ]$

5. $\quad 7x - 1 = 2x + 5$
    $\quad -[\ ] \qquad -2x$
    $\overline{\quad 5x - 1 = [\ ]}$
    $\quad +[\ ] \quad +1$
    $\overline{\qquad 5x = [\ ]}$
    $\quad \dfrac{5x}{[\ ]} = \dfrac{6}{[\ ]}$
    $\qquad x = [\ ]$

6. $\quad -3r + 9 = -4r + 5$
    $\quad +[\ ] \qquad +4r$
    $\overline{\quad r + 9 = 5}$
    $\qquad -[\ ] \quad -9$
    $\overline{\qquad r = [\ ]}$

Solve.

7. $3y + 1 = 4y - 6$
8. $2 + 6x = 1 - x$
9. $5y + 4 = 4y + 5$

_____ _____ _____

Write an equation to represent each relationship. Then solve the equation.

10. Ten less than 3 times a number is the same as the number plus 4.

_____

11. Six times a number plus 4 is the same as the number minus 11.

_____

12. Fifteen more than twice the hours Carla worked last week is the same as three times the hours she worked this week decreased by 15. She worked the same number of hours each week. How many hours did she work each week?

_____

Original content Copyright © by Houghton Mifflin Harcourt. Additions and changes to the original content are the responsibility of the instructor.

Name _____ Date _____ Class _____

LESSON 7-1

Equations with the Variable on Both Sides
Reteach

If there are variable terms on both sides of an equation, first collect them on one side. Do this by adding or subtracting. When possible, collect the variables on the side of the equation where the coefficient will be positive.

Solve the equation $5x = 2x + 12$. $\quad 5x = 2x + 12$ $\quad \underline{-2x \quad -2x}$ $\quad 3x = 12$ $\quad \dfrac{3x}{3} = \dfrac{12}{3}$ $\quad x = 4$	To collect on left side, subtract $2x$ from both sides of the equation. Divide by 3.	**Check:** Substitute into the original equation. $5x = 2x + 12$ $5(4) \stackrel{?}{=} 2(4) + 12$ $20 \stackrel{?}{=} 8 + 12$ $20 = 20$
Solve the equation $-6z + 28 = 9z - 2$ $\quad -6z + 28 = 9z - 2$ $\quad \underline{+6z \quad\quad +6z}$ $\quad\quad 28 = 15z - 2$ $\quad \underline{+2 \quad\quad +2}$ $\quad\quad 30 = 15z$ $\quad\quad \dfrac{30}{15} = \dfrac{15z}{15}$ $\quad\quad 2 = z$	To collect on right side, add $6z$ to both sides of the equation. Add 2 to both sides of the equation. Divide by 15.	**Check:** Substitute into the original equation. $-6z + 28 = 9z - 2$ $-6(2) + 28 \stackrel{?}{=} 9(2) - 2$ $-12 + 28 \stackrel{?}{=} 18 - 2$ $16 = 16$

Complete to solve and check each equation.

1. $9m + 2 = 3m - 10$

   $\quad 9m + 2 = 3m - 10$
   $\quad \underline{-[\ ] \quad\quad -[\ ]}$
   $\quad 6m + 2 = \quad -10$
   $\quad \underline{-[\ ] \quad\quad -[\ ]}$
   $\quad 6m = [\ ]$
   $\quad \dfrac{6m}{[\ ]} = \dfrac{-12}{[\ ]}$
   $\quad m = [\ ]$

   To collect on left side, subtract ____ from both sides.

   Subtract ____ from both sides.

   Divide by ____.

   Check: Substitute into the original equation.
   $9m + 2 = 3m - 10$
   $9(\underline{\ \ }) + 2 \stackrel{?}{=} 3(\underline{\ \ }) - 10$
   $\underline{\ \ } + 2 \stackrel{?}{=} \underline{\ \ } - 10$
   $\underline{\ \ } = \underline{\ \ }$

2. $-7d - 22 = 4d$

   $\quad -7d - 22 = 4d$
   $\quad \underline{+[\ ] \quad\quad +[\ ]}$
   $\quad\quad -22 = 11d$
   $\quad \dfrac{-22}{[\ ]} = \dfrac{11d}{[\ ]}$
   $\quad [\ ] = d$

   To collect on right side, add ____ to both sides.

   Divide by ____.

   Check: Substitute into the original equation.
   $-7d - 22 = 4d$
   $-7(\underline{\ \ }) - 22 \stackrel{?}{=} 4(\underline{\ \ })$
   $\underline{\ \ } - 22 \stackrel{?}{=} \underline{\ \ }$
   $\underline{\ \ } = \underline{\ \ }$

Name _____ Date _____ Class _____

LESSON 7-2 Equations with Rational Numbers
Practice and Problem Solving: A/B

Write the least common multiple of the denominators in the equation.

1. $9 + \dfrac{3}{4}x = \dfrac{7}{8}x - 10$ _____

2. $\dfrac{2}{3}x + \dfrac{1}{6} = -\dfrac{3}{4}x + 1$ _____

Describe the operations used to solve the equation.

3. $\dfrac{5}{6}x - 2 = -\dfrac{2}{3}x + 1$

$6\left(\dfrac{5}{6}x - 2\right) = 6\left(-\dfrac{2}{3}x + 1\right)$ _____

$5x - 12 = -4x + 6$ _____

$\underline{+4x \qquad\quad +4x}$ _____

$9x - 12 = \quad\ 6$ _____

$\underline{+12 \qquad +12}$ _____

$9x = 18$ _____

$\dfrac{9x}{9} = \dfrac{18}{9}$ _____

$x = 2$ _____

Solve.

4. $\dfrac{2}{3}x + \dfrac{1}{3} = \dfrac{1}{3}x + \dfrac{2}{3}$

_____

5. $\dfrac{3}{5}n + \dfrac{9}{10} = -\dfrac{1}{5}n - \dfrac{23}{10}$

_____

6. $\dfrac{5}{6}h - \dfrac{7}{12} = -\dfrac{3}{4}h - \dfrac{13}{6}$

_____

7. $4.5w = 5.1w - 30$

_____

8. $\dfrac{4}{7}y - 2 = \dfrac{3}{7}y + \dfrac{3}{14}$

_____

9. $-0.8a - 8 = 0.2a$

_____

10. Write and solve a real-world problem that can be modeled by the equation $0.75x - 18.50 = 0.65x$.

_____

_____

_____

Name _____ Date _____ Class _____

LESSON 7-2
Equations with Rational Numbers
Reteach

To solve an equation with a variable on both sides that involves fractions, first get rid of the fractions.

Solve $\frac{3}{4}m + 2 = \frac{2}{3}m + 5$.

$12\left(\frac{3}{4}m + 2\right) = 12\left(\frac{2}{3}m + 5\right)$

$12\left(\frac{3}{4}m\right) + 12(2) = 12\left(\frac{2}{3}m\right) + 12(5)$

$9m + 24 = 8m + 60$
$\underline{-8m \quad\quad -8m}$
$m + 24 = 60$
$\underline{\quad -24 \quad\quad -24}$
$m = 36$

Multiply both sides of the equation by 12, the LCM of 4 and 3.

Multiply each term by 12.
Simplify.
Subtract 8m from both sides.
Simplify.
Subtract 24 from both sides.
Simplify.

Check: Substitute into the original equation.

$\frac{3}{4}m + 2 = \frac{2}{3}m + 5$

$\frac{3}{4}(36) + 2 \stackrel{?}{=} \frac{2}{3}(36) + 5$

$27 + 2 \stackrel{?}{=} 24 + 5$

$29 = 29$

Complete to solve and check your answer.

1. $\frac{1}{4}x + 2 = \frac{2}{5}x - 1$

[ ]$\left(\frac{1}{4}x + 2\right) = $ [ ]$\left(\frac{2}{5}x - 1\right)$

[ ]$\left(\frac{1}{4}x\right) + $ [ ]$(2) = $ [ ]$\left(\frac{2}{5}x\right) - $ [ ](1)

[ ]$x + $ [ ] $= $ [ ]$x - $ [ ]
$\underline{-5x \quad\quad\quad -5x}$
$40 = 3x - 20$
$\underline{+20 \quad\quad +20}$
[ ] $= 3x$

$\frac{60}{[\ ]} = \frac{3x}{[\ ]}$

[ ] $= x$

Multiply both sides of the equation by ___, the LCM of 4 and 5.

Multiply each term by ___.

Simplify.
Subtract ___.
Simplify.
Add ___.
Simplify.
Divide both sides by ___.

Simplify.

Check: Substitute into the original equation.

$\frac{1}{4}x + 2 = \frac{2}{5}x - 1$

$\frac{1}{4}(\_\_) + 2 \stackrel{?}{=} \frac{2}{5}(\_\_) - 1$

$\_\_ + 2 \stackrel{?}{=} \_\_ - 1$

$\_\_ = \_\_$

Name _____ Date _____ Class _____

LESSON 7-3 Equations with the Distributive Property
Practice and Problem Solving: A/B

Solve each equation.

1. $4(x - 2) = x + 10$

2. $\frac{2}{3}(n - 6) = 5n - 43$

3. $-2(y + 12) = y - 9$

4. $8(12 - k) = 3(k + 21)$

5. $8(-1 + m) + 3 = 2\left(m - 5\frac{1}{2}\right)$

6. $2y - 3(2y - 3) + 2 = 31$

Use the situation below to complete Exercises 7–8.

A taxi company charges $2.25 for the first mile and then $0.20 per mile for each additional mile, or $F = \$2.25 + \$0.20(m - 1)$ where F is the fare and m is the number of miles.

7. If Juan's taxi fare was $6.05, how many miles did he travel in the taxi?

8. If Juan's taxi fare was $7.65, how many miles did he travel in the taxi?

Use the situation below to complete Exercises 9–11.

The equation used to estimate typing speed is $S = \frac{1}{5}(w - 10e)$, where S is the accurate typing speed, w is the number of words typed in 5 minutes and e is the number of errors.

9. Ignacio can type 55 words per minute (wpm). In 5 minutes, she types 285 words. How many errors would you expect her to make?

10. If Alexis types 300 words in 5 minutes with 5 errors, what is his typing speed?

11. Johanna receives a report that says her typing speed is 65 words per minute. She knows that she made 4 errors in the 5-minute test. How many words did she type in 5 minutes?

Original content Copyright © by Houghton Mifflin Harcourt. Additions and changes to the original content are the responsibility of the instructor.

LESSON 7-3 Equations with the Distributive Property
Reteach

When solving an equation, it is important to simplify on both sides of the equal sign before you try to isolate the variable.

$3(x + 4) + 2 = x + 10$ — Since you cannot combine x and 4, multiply both by 3 using the Distributive Property.
$3x + 12 + 2 = x + 10$ — Then combine like terms.
$3x + 14 = x + 10$
$\quad -14 \quad\quad -14$ — Subtract 14 to begin to isolate the variable term.
$3x = x - 4$
$-x \quad -x$ — Subtract x to get the variables to one side of the equation.
$\dfrac{2x}{2} = \dfrac{-4}{2}$ — Divide by 2 to isolate the variable.
$x = -2$ — The solution is -2.

Solve.

1. $5(i + 2) - 9 = -17 - i$

2. $-3(n + 2) = n - 22$

You may need to distribute on both sides of the equal sign before simplifying.

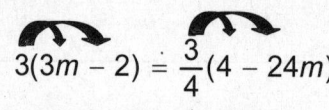
$3(3m - 2) = \dfrac{3}{4}(4 - 24m)$ — Use the Distributive Property on both sides of the equation to remove the parentheses.
$9m - 6 = 3 - 18m$
$\quad +6 \quad +6$ — Add 6 to begin to isolate the variable term.
$9m = 9 - 18m$
$+18m \quad +18m$ — Add $18m$ to get the variables to one side of the equation.
$\dfrac{27m}{27} = \dfrac{9}{27}$ — Divide by 27 to isolate the variable.
$m = \dfrac{1}{3}$ — The solution is $\dfrac{1}{3}$.

Solve.

3. $9(y - 4) = -10\left(y + 2\dfrac{1}{3}\right)$

4. $-7\left(-6 - \dfrac{6}{7}x\right) = 12\left(x - 3\dfrac{1}{2}\right)$

Name _____ Date _____ Class _____

LESSON 7-4
Equations with Many Solutions or No Solution
Practice and Problem Solving: A/B

**Tell whether each equation has one, zero, or infinitely many solutions.
If the equation has one solution, solve the equation.**

1. $4(x-2) = 4x + 10$

2. $\frac{1}{2}n + 7 = \frac{n+14}{2}$

3. $6(x-1) = 6x - 1$

4. $6n + 7 - 2n - 14 = 5n + 1$

5. $4x + 5 = 9 + 4x$

6. $\frac{1}{2}(8-x) = \frac{8-x}{2}$

7. $8(y+4) = 7y + 38$

8. $4(-8x + 12) = -26 - 32x$

9. $2(x+12) = 3x + 24 - x$

10. $3x - 14 + 2(x-9) = 2x - 2$

Solve.

11. Cell phone company A charges $20 per month plus $0.05 per text message. Cell phone company B charges $10 per month plus $0.07 per text message. Is there any number of text messages that will result in the exact same charge from both companies?

12. Lisa's pet shop has 2 fish tanks. Tank A contains smaller fish who are fed 1 gram of food each per day. Tank B contains larger fish who are fed 2 grams of food each per day. If Tank B contains $\frac{2}{3}$ the number of fish that Tank A contains, will Lisa ever feed both tanks the same amount of food?

Name _____ Date _____ Class _____

LESSON 7-4
Equations with Many Solutions or No Solution
Reteach

When you solve a linear equation, you are trying to find a value for the variable that makes the equation true. Often there is only one value that makes an equation true – one solution. But sometimes there is no value that will make the equation true. Other times there are many values that make the equation true.

$x + 3 = 8$
$x = 5$

Use properties of equality to solve.
If you get a statement that tells you what the variable equals, the equation has **one solution**.

$x + 3 = x + 4$
$3 = 4$

If you get a false statement with no variables, the equation has **no solution**.

$x + 3 = x + 3$
$3 = 3$

If you get a true statement with no variables, the equation has infinitely **many solutions**.

Tell whether each equation has one, zero, or infinitely many solutions.

1. $5(i + 2) = 8(i - 1)$

2. $-3(n + 2) = -3n - 6$

_____   _____

You can write an equation with one solution, no solution, or infinitely many solutions.

One solution: Start with a variable on one side and a constant on the other. This is your solution. Add, subtract, multiply or divide both sides of the equation by the same constant(s). Your equation has one solution. **Example:** $3(r + 2) = 30$

No solution: Start with a false statement of equality about two constants, such as $3 = 4$. Now add, subtract, multiply or divide the same variable from both sides. You may then add, subtract, multiply or divide additional constants to both sides. Your equation has no solution. **Example:** $k + 3 = k + 4$

Infinitely many solutions: Start with a true statement of equality about two constants, such as $5 = 5$. Now add, subtract, multiply or divide the same variable from both sides. You may then add, subtract, multiply or divide additional constants to both sides. Your equation has many solutions. **Example:** $5(n - 3) = 5n - 15$

Solve.

3. Write an equation with one solution. _____

4. Write an equation with no solution. _____

5. Write an equation with infinitely many solutions. _____

Name _____ Date _____ Class _____

LESSON 8-1
Solving Systems of Linear Equations by Graphing
Practice and Problem Solving: A/B

Solve each linear system by graphing. Check your answer.

1. $y = -1$
   $y = 2x - 7$

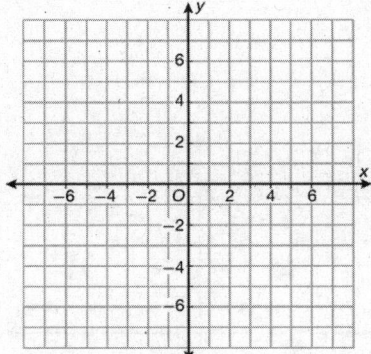

2. $x - y = 6$
   $2x = 12 + 2y$

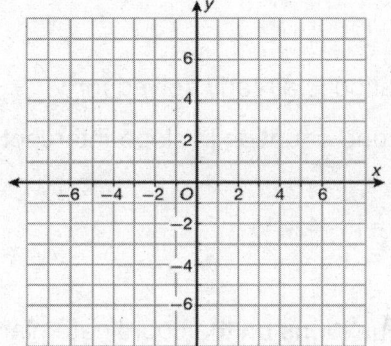

3. $\frac{1}{2}x - y = 4$
   $2y = x + 6$

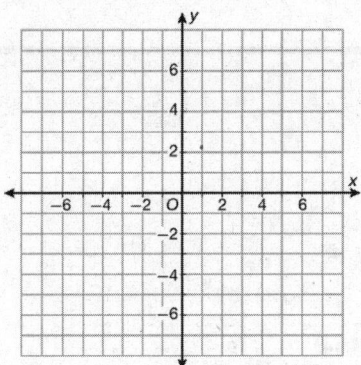

4. $y = 4x - 3$
   $2y - 3x = 4$

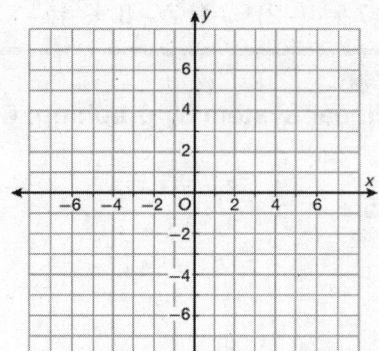

5. Two skaters are racing toward the finish line of a race. The first skater has a 40 meter lead and is traveling at a rate of 12 meters per second. The second skater is traveling at a rate of 14 meters per second. How long will it take for the second skater to pass the first skater?

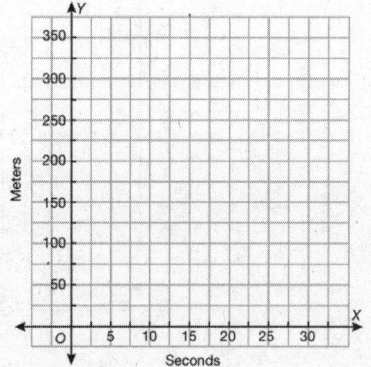

Original content Copyright © by Houghton Mifflin Harcourt. Additions and changes to the original content are the responsibility of the instructor.

LESSON 8-1 Solving Systems of Linear Equations by Graphing
Reteach

When solving a system of linear equations by graphing, first write each equation in slope-intercept form. Do this by solving each equation for y.

Solve the following system of equations by graphing.

$y = -2x + 3$
$y + 4x = -1$

The first equation is already solved for y.

Write the second equation in slope-intercept form. Solve for y.

$y + 4x - 4x = -1 - 4x$

$y = -4x - 1$

Graph both equations on the coordinate plane.

The lines intersect at $(-2, 7)$. This is the solution to the system of linear equations.

To check the answer, substitute -2 for x and 7 for y in the original equations.

$y = -2x + 3;\ 7 = -2(-2) + 3;\ 7 = 4 + 3;\ 7 = 7$
$y + 4x = -1;\ 7 + 4(-2) = -1;\ 7 - 8 = -1;\ -1 = -1$

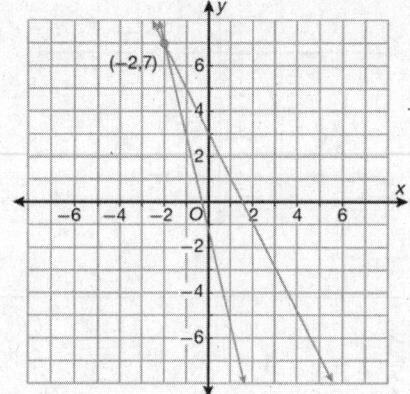

Solve each linear system by graphing. Check your answer.

1. $y = x + 1$
   $y = -x + 5$

2. $y + 3x = 1$
   $y - 6 = 2x$

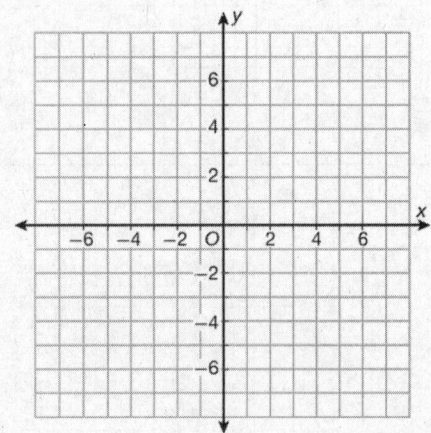
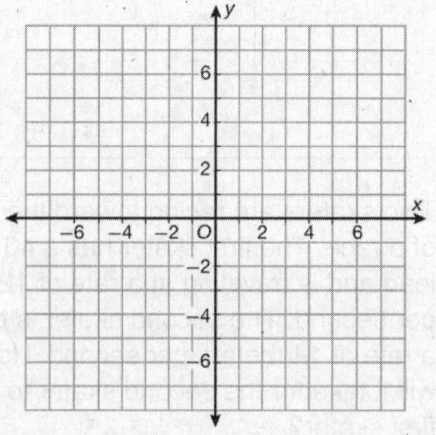

Name _____ Date _____ Class _____

LESSON 8-2
Solving Systems by Substitution
Practice and Problem Solving: A/B

Solve each system by substitution. Check your answer.

1. $\begin{cases} y = x - 2 \\ y = 4x + 1 \end{cases}$

2. $\begin{cases} 2x - y = 6 \\ x + y = -3 \end{cases}$

3. $\begin{cases} 3x - 2y = 7 \\ x + 3y = -5 \end{cases}$

(_____ , _____) (_____ , _____) (_____ , _____)

Estimate the solution of each system by sketching its graph.

4. $\begin{cases} x = -\dfrac{1}{4}y + 5 \\ 3x + 2y = 0 \end{cases}$

5. $\begin{cases} 3x = -y + 10 \\ 2x + 3y = -12 \end{cases}$

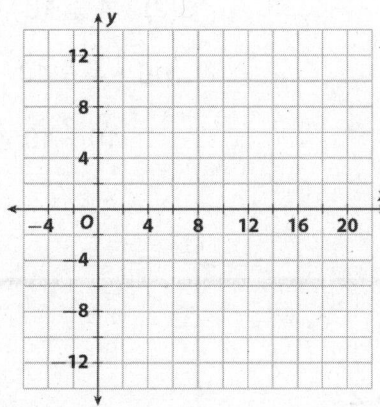   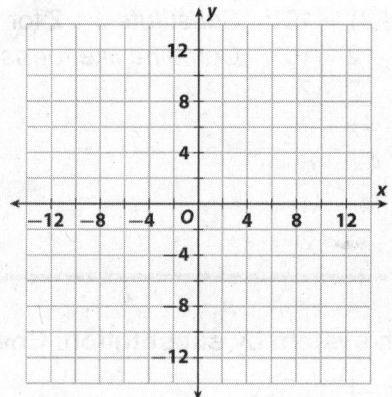

Estimated solution: Estimated solution:

(about _____ , about _____)   (about _____ , about _____)

6. A sales associate in a department store earns a commission on each suit and each pair of shoes sold. One week, she earned $47 in commission for selling 3 suits and a pair of shoes. The next week, she earned $107 in commission for selling 7 suits and 2 pairs of shoes. How much commission does she earn for selling each suit and each pair of shoes? Solve by substitution.

_____

LESSON 8-2
Solving Systems by Substitution
Reteach

You can use substitution to solve a system of equations if one of the equations is already solved for a variable.

Solve $\begin{cases} y = x + 2 \\ 3x + y = 10 \end{cases}$

Step 1: Choose the equation to use as the substitute.
Use the first equation $y = x + 2$ because it is already solved for a variable.

Step 2: Solve by substitution.

$3x + y = 10$
$3x + (x + 2) = 10$ *Substitute $x + 2$ for y.*
$4x + 2 = 10$ *Combine like terms.*
$\underline{ -2 -2}$
$4x = 8$
$\dfrac{4x}{4} = \dfrac{8}{4}$
$x = 2$

Step 3: Now substitute $x = 2$ back into one of the original equations to find the value of y.

$y = x + 2$
$y = 2 + 2$
$y = 4$

The solution is $(2, 4)$.

Check:
Substitute $(2, 4)$ into both equations.

$y = x + 2$ $3x + y = 10$
$4 \stackrel{?}{=} 2 + 2$ $3(2) + 4 \stackrel{?}{=} 10$
$4 \stackrel{?}{=} 4$ ✓ $6 + 4 \stackrel{?}{=} 10$
                   $10 \stackrel{?}{=} 10$ ✓

Solve each system by substitution. Check your answer.

1. $\begin{cases} x = y - 1 \\ x + 2y = 8 \end{cases}$

2. $\begin{cases} y = x + 2 \\ y = 2x - 5 \end{cases}$

3. $\begin{cases} y = x + 5 \\ 3x + y = -11 \end{cases}$

4. $\begin{cases} x = y + 10 \\ x = 2y + 3 \end{cases}$

Name _____ Date _____ Class _____

LESSON 8-3 Solving Systems by Elimination
Practice and Problem Solving: A/B

Solve each system by eliminating one of the variables by addition or subtraction. Check your answer.

1. $\begin{cases} x - y = 8 \\ x + y = 12 \end{cases}$

2. $\begin{cases} 2x - y = 4 \\ 3x + y = 6 \end{cases}$

3. $\begin{cases} x + 2y = 10 \\ x + 4y = 14 \end{cases}$

(_____, _____)   (_____, _____)   (_____, _____)

4. $\begin{cases} 3x + y = 9 \\ y = 3x + 6 \end{cases}$

5. $\begin{cases} 4x + 5y = 15 \\ 6x - 5y = 18 \end{cases}$

6. $\begin{cases} 5x = 7y \\ x + 7y = 21 \end{cases}$

(_____, _____)   (_____, _____)   (_____, _____)

Write a system of equations for each problem. Solve the system using elimination. Show your work and check your answers.

7. Aaron bought a bagel and 3 muffins for $7.25. Bea bought a bagel and 2 muffins for $6. How much is a bagel and how much is a muffin?

_____

8. Two movie tickets and 3 snacks are $24. Three movie tickets and 4 snacks are $35. How much is a movie ticket and how much is a snack.

_____

Explain why the system has the answer given. Solve each system by elimination to prove your answer.

9. $\begin{cases} x + 2y = 8 \\ x + 2y = 20 \end{cases}$

   No solution

10. $\begin{cases} 3x + y = 9 \\ 3x = 9 - y \end{cases}$

    Infinitely many solutions

_____   _____

_____   _____

Name _____ Date _____ Class _____

LESSON 8-3
Solving Systems by Elimination
Reteach

Solving a system of two equations in two unknowns by **elimination** can be done by adding or subtracting one equation from the other.

Elimination by Adding
Solve the system: $x + 4y = 8$
$\quad\quad\quad\quad\quad\quad\quad\quad 3x - 4y = 8$

Solution
Notice that the terms "+4y" and "−4y" are opposites. This means that the two equations can be added without changing the signs.
$$x + 4y = 8$$
$$\underline{3x - 4y = 8}$$
$$4x + 0 = 16$$
$$4x = 16, \text{ or } x = 4$$

Substitute $x = 4$ in either of the equations to find y: $x + 4y = 8 \longrightarrow 4 + 4y = 8$
$$4y = 4, \text{ or}$$
$$y = 1$$

The solution of this system is (4, 1).

Elimination by Subtracting
Solve the system: $2x - 5y = 15$
$\quad\quad\quad\quad\quad\quad\quad\quad 2x + 3y = -9$

Solution
Notice that the terms "2x" are common to both equations. However, to eliminate them, it is necessary to *subtract* one equation from the other. This means that the *signs* of one equation will change. Here, the top equation stays the same. The signs of the bottom equation change.

$$2x - 5y = 15$$
$$\underline{(-)2x (-)3y = (+)9}$$
$$0 - 8y = 24, \text{ or } y = -3$$

Substitute $y = -3$ in either of the original equations to find x:
$2x - 5y = 15 \longrightarrow 2x - 5(-3) = 15$
$$2x + 15 = 15, \text{ or}$$
$$x = 0$$

The solution of this system is (0, −3).

Solve the following systems by elimination. State whether addition or subtraction is used to eliminate one of the variables.

1. $3x + 2y = 10$
   $3x - 2y = 14$

   Operation: _____

   Solution: (_____, _____)

2. $\begin{cases} x + y = 12 \\ 2x + y = 6 \end{cases}$

   Operation: _____

   Solution: (_____, _____)

Name _____ Date _____ Class _____

LESSON 8-4 Solving Systems by Elimination with Multiplication
Practice and Problem Solving: A/B

Name the *least common multiple* (LCM) of the coefficients of each pair of variables. Ignore the signs.

1. $\begin{cases} -2a + 3b = 9 \\ 4a - 2b = 3 \end{cases}$

    LCM for *a*: _____
    LCM for *b*: _____

2. $\begin{cases} 7x + 5y = 20 \\ 6x - 18y = 11 \end{cases}$

    LCM for *x*: _____
    LCM for *y*: _____

3. $\begin{cases} -8m - 5n = 3 \\ 3m - 12n = -1 \end{cases}$

    LCM for *m*: _____
    LCM for *n*: _____

Solve each system by elimination, multiplication, and addition or subtraction. Show and check your work.

4. $\begin{cases} x + 3y = -14 \\ 2x - 4y = 30 \end{cases}$

5. $\begin{cases} 4x - y = -5 \\ -2x + 3y = 10 \end{cases}$

6. $\begin{cases} y - 3x = 11 \\ 2y - x = 2 \end{cases}$

(____, ____)   (____, ____)   (____, ____)

Write and solve a system of linear equations for each problem. Show and check your work.

7. One family spends $134 on 2 adult tickets and 3 youth tickets at an amusement park. Another family spends $146 on 3 adult tickets and 2 youth tickets at the same park. What is the price of a youth ticket?

_____

_____

8. A baker buys 19 apples of two different varieties to make pies. The total cost of the apples is $5.10. Granny Smith apples cost $0.25 each and Gala apples cost $0.30. How many of each type of apple did the baker buy?

_____

_____

Original content Copyright © by Houghton Mifflin Harcourt. Additions and changes to the original content are the responsibility of the instructor.

LESSON 8-4: Solving Systems by Elimination with Multiplication
Reteach

Elimination is used to solve a system of equations by adding like terms. Sometimes, it is necessary to multiply one or both equations by a number to use this method. You should examine the equations carefully and choose the coefficients that are easiest to eliminate.

Multiplying *one* equation by a number

$\begin{cases} 2x + 5y = 9 \\ x - 3y = 10 \end{cases}$

The easiest variable to work with is *x*. Multiply the second equation by –2.

$2x + 5y = 9$
$-2(x - 3y) = -2(10)$

$2x + 5y = 9$
$-2x + 6y = -20$
$\overline{0 + 11y = -11}$

So, $y = -1$, and $2x + 5(-1) = 9$, or $x = 7$. The solution is (7, –1).

Multiplying *both* equations by a number

$\begin{cases} 5x + 3y = 2 \\ 4x + 2y = 10 \end{cases}$

The *least common multiple* (LCM) of 4 and 5 is 20, and the LCM of 2 and 3 is 6. So, multiply the first equation by –2 and the second equation by 3.

$-2(5x + 3y = 2)$
$3(4x + 2y = 10)$

$-10x - 6y = -4$
$12x + 6y = 30$
$\overline{2x + 0 = 26}$

So, $x = 13$, and $5(13) + 3y = 2$, so $y = -21$. The solution is (13, –21).

Solve each system by elimination.

1. $\begin{cases} 2x - y = 20 \\ 3x + 2y = 19 \end{cases}$

2. $\begin{cases} -3a + 4b = 15 \\ 5a - 6b = 12 \end{cases}$

(_____, _____)   (_____, _____)

3. $\begin{cases} 3m + 5n = 20 \\ 4m - 6n = 30 \end{cases}$

4. $\begin{cases} 3u - v = 20 \\ -4u - 2v = 13 \end{cases}$

(_____, _____)   (_____, _____)

Name _____ Date _____ Class _____

LESSON 8-5
Solving Special Systems
Practice and Problem Solving: A/B

Graph each system. Describe the solution.

1. $\begin{cases} y = x + 2 \\ x - y = 2 \end{cases}$

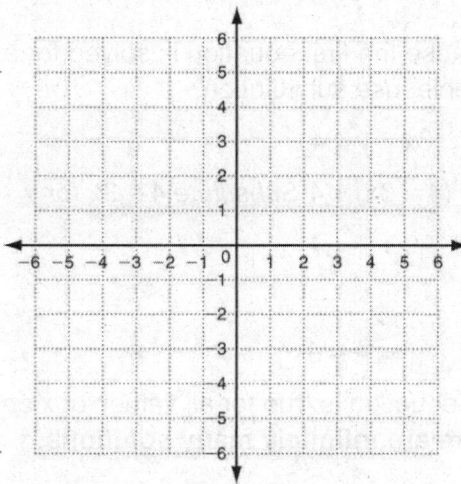

Solution:
_____

2. $\begin{cases} x + 2y = 5 \\ 3x = 15 - 6y \end{cases}$

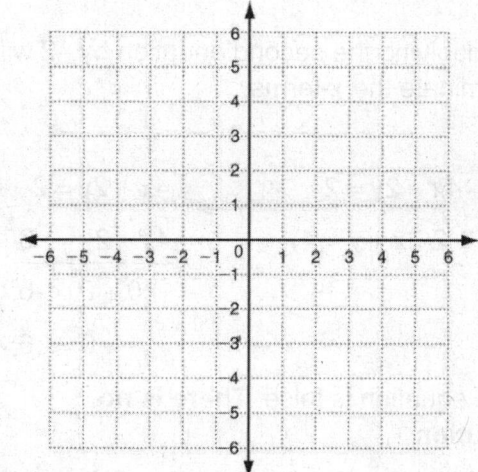

Solution:
_____

Re-write each system in the form $y = mx + b$. Then, state whether the system has one solution, no solution, or many solutions without actually solving the system.

3. $\begin{cases} 2x + y = 1 \\ 2x + y = -3 \end{cases}$

4. $\begin{cases} y - 2 = -5x \\ y - 5x = 2 \end{cases}$

5. $\begin{cases} y - 3x + 2 = 0 \\ 2 = -y + 3x \end{cases}$

_____ _____ _____

Solve.

6. Two sisters open savings accounts with $60 each that their grandmother gave them. The first sister adds $20 each month to her account. The second sister adds $40 every two months to her $60. If the sisters continue to make deposits at the same rate, when will they have the same amount of money?

_____

Name _____ Date _____ Class _____

LESSON 8-5
Solving Special Systems
Reteach

When solving equations in one variable, it is possible to have one solution, no solutions, or infinitely many solutions. The same results can occur when graphing systems of equations.

Solve $\begin{cases} 4x + 2y = 2 \\ 2x + y = 4 \end{cases}$

Solve $\begin{cases} y = 4 - 3x \\ 3x + y = 4 \end{cases}$

Multiplying the second equation by −2 will eliminate the *x*-terms.

$4x + 2y = 2$ → $4x + 2y = 2$
$-2(2x + y = 4)$ $-4x - 2y = -8$
                     $0 + 0 = -6$
                     $0 = -6$ ✗

The equation is false. **There is no solution.**

Because the first equation is solved for a variable, use substitution.

$3x + y = 4$
$3x + (4 - 3x) = 4$ Substitute $4 - 3x$ for *y*
$0 + 4 = 4$

$4 = 4$ ✓

The equation is true for all values of *x* and *y*. **There are infinitely many solutions.**

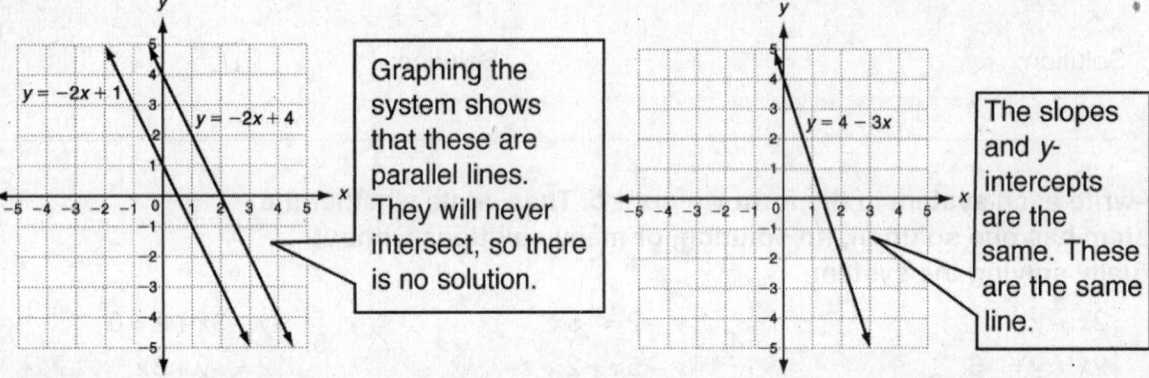

Graphing the system shows that these are parallel lines. They will never intersect, so there is no solution.

The slopes and *y*-intercepts are the same. These are the same line.

Solve each system of linear equations algebraically.

1. $\begin{cases} y = 3x \\ 2y = 6x \end{cases}$

2. $\begin{cases} y = 2x + 5 \\ y - 2x = 1 \end{cases}$

3. $\begin{cases} 3x - 2y = 9 \\ -6x + 4y = 1 \end{cases}$

_____ _____ _____

Name _____ Date _____ Class _____

LESSON 9-1 Properties of Translations
Practice and Problem Solving: A/B

Describe the translation that maps point A to point A'.

1.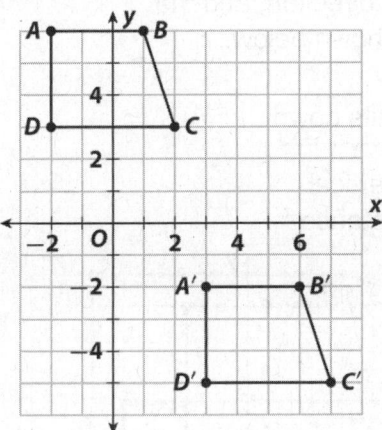

2.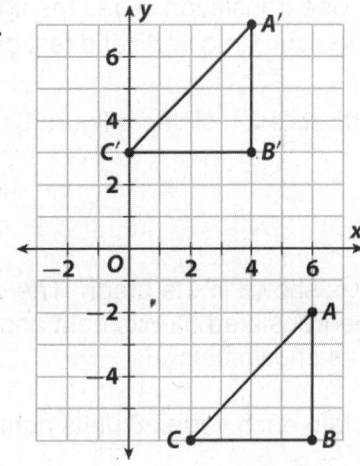

_____   _____

Draw the image of the figure after each translation.

3. 3 units left and 9 units down

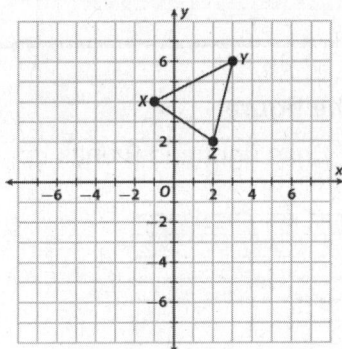

4. 3 units right and 6 units up

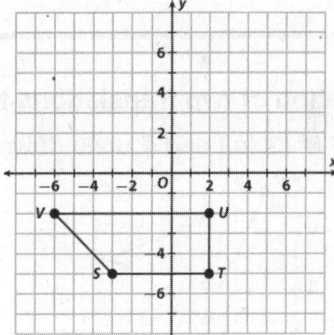

5. a. Graph rectangle J'K'L'M', the image of rectangle JKLM, after a translation of 1 unit right and 9 units up.

   b. Find the area of each rectangle.

   _____

   c. Is it possible for the area of a figure to change after it is translated? Explain.

   _____

   _____

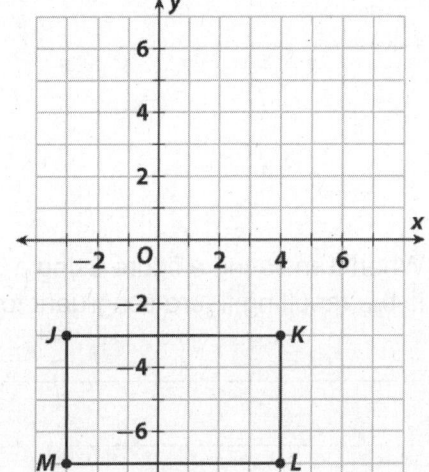

Name _____ Date _____ Class _____

LESSON 9-1 Properties of Translations
Reteach

The description of a translation in a coordinate plane uses a combination of two translations – one translation slides the figure in a horizontal direction, and the other slides the figure in a vertical direction. An example is shown below.

A translation slides a figure 8 units right and 5 units down.
  horizontal distance vertical distance

Triangle *LMN* is shown in the graph. The triangle can be translated 8 units right and 5 units down as shown below.

Step 1 Translate each vertex 8 units right.

Step 2 Translate each vertex 5 units down.

Step 3 Label the resulting vertices and connect them to form triangle *L'M'N'*.

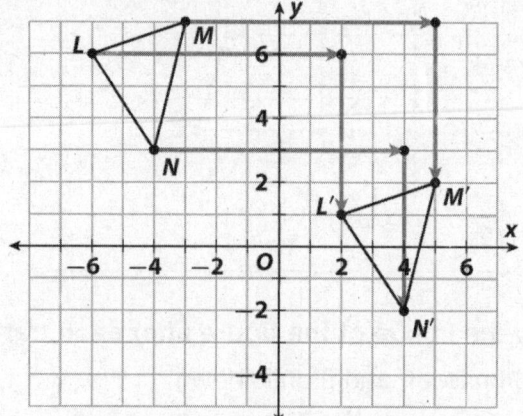

Use a combination of two translations to draw the image of the figure.

1. Translate 6 units left and 7 units down.

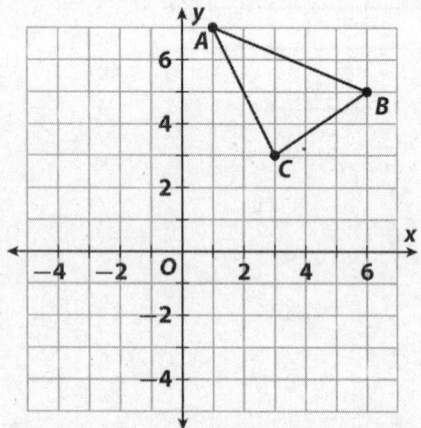

2. Translate 7 units right and 9 units up.

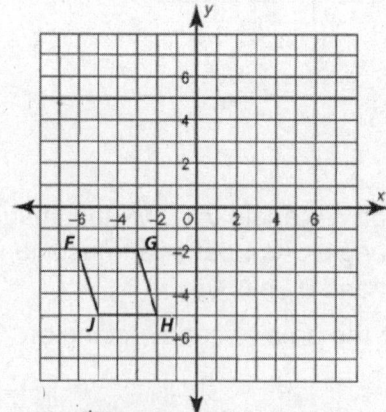

3. When translating a figure using a combination of two translations, is the resulting figure congruent to the original figure? Explain.

_____

_____

Name _____ Date _____ Class_____

LESSON 9-2
Properties of Reflections
Practice and Problem Solving: A/B

Use the graph for Exercises 1–3.

1. Quadrilateral J is reflected across the x-axis. What is the image of the reflection?

   _____

2. Which two quadrilaterals are reflections of each other across the y-axis?

   _____

3. How are quadrilaterals H and J related?

   _____

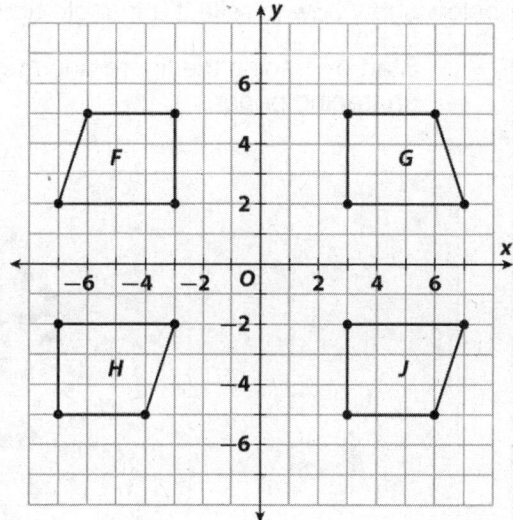

Draw the image of the figure after each reflection.

4. across the x-axis

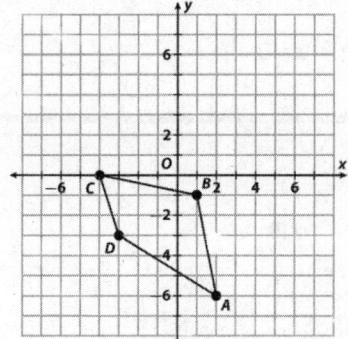

5. across the y-axis

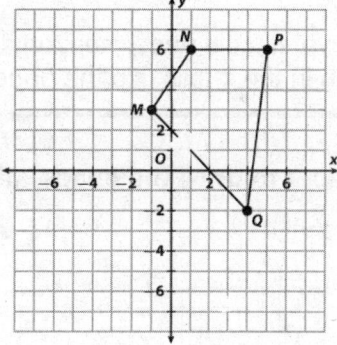

6. a. Graph rectangle K'L'M'N', the image of rectangle KLMN after a reflection across the y-axis.

    b. What is the perimeter of each rectangle?

    _____

    c. Is it possible for the perimeter of a figure to change after it is reflected? Explain.

    _____

    _____

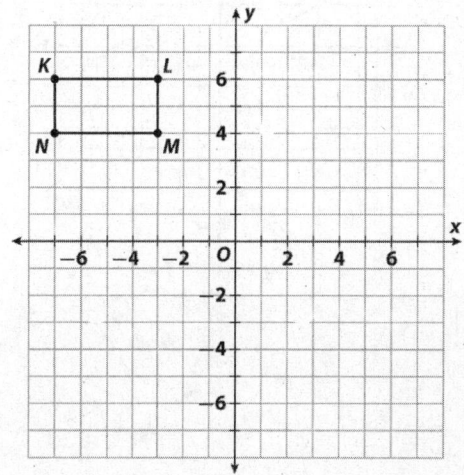

Original content Copyright © by Houghton Mifflin Harcourt. Additions and changes to the original content are the responsibility of the instructor.

Name _____ Date _____ Class _____

LESSON 9-2 Properties of Reflections
Reteach

You can use tracing paper to reflect a figure in the coordinate plane. The graphs below show how to reflect a triangle across the y-axis.

Start by tracing the figure and the axes on tracing paper.

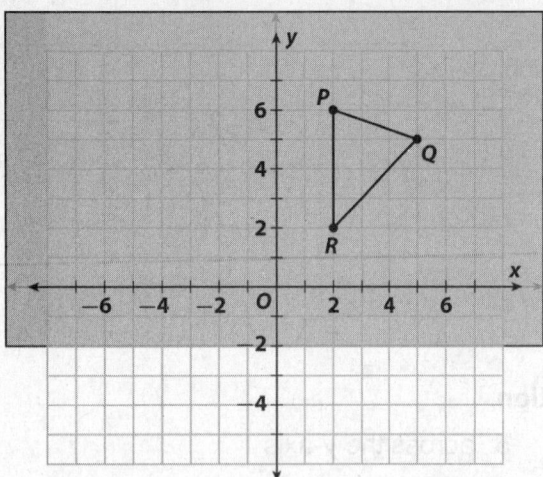

Flip the tracing paper over, making sure to align the axes. Transfer the flipped image onto the coordinate plane.

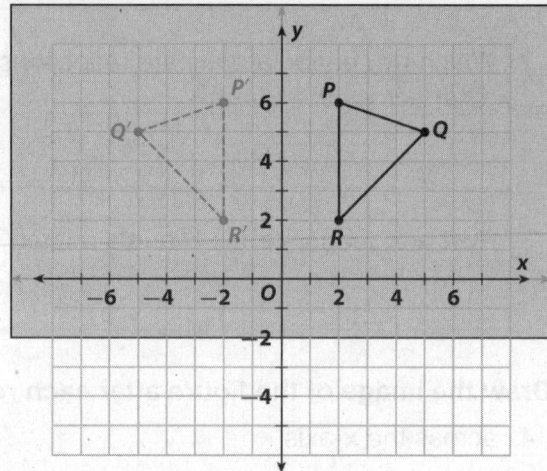

As shown above, flip the paper horizontally for a reflection in the y-axis. For a reflection in the x-axis, flip the paper vertically.

Use tracing paper to draw the image after the reflection.

1. across the y-axis

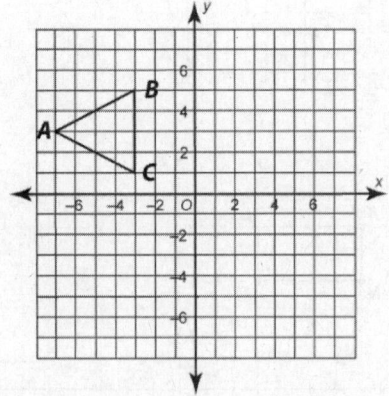

2. across the x-axis

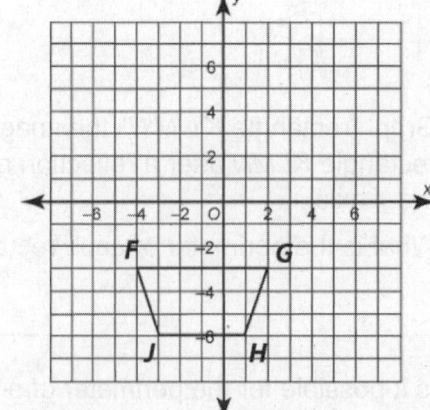

Original content Copyright © by Houghton Mifflin Harcourt. Additions and changes to the original content are the responsibility of the instructor.

Name _____ Date _____ Class _____

LESSON 9-3 Properties of Rotations
Practice and Problem Solving: A/B

Use the figures at the right for Exercises 1–5. Triangle A has been rotated about the origin.

1. Which triangle shows a 90° counterclockwise rotation? ____

2. Which triangle shows a 180° counterclockwise rotation? ____

3. Which triangle shows a 270° clockwise rotation? ____

4. Which triangle shows a 270° counterclockwise rotation? ____

5. If the sides of triangle A have lengths of 30 cm, 40 cm, and 50 cm, what are the lengths of the sides of triangle D?

   _____

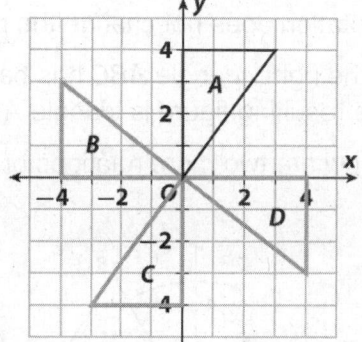

Use the figures at the right for Exercises 6–10. Figure A is to be rotated about the origin.

6. If you rotate figure A 90° counterclockwise, what quadrant will the image be in? ____

7. If you rotate figure A 270° counterclockwise, what quadrant will the image be in? ____

8. If you rotate figure A 180° clockwise, what quadrant will the image be in? ____

9. If you rotate figure A 360° clockwise, what quadrant will the image be in? ____

10. If the measures of two angles in figure A are 60° and 120°, what will the measure of those two angles be in the rotated figure?

    _____

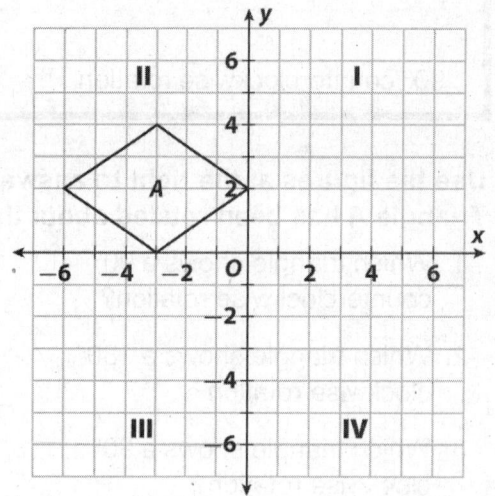

Use the grid at the right for Exercises 11–12.

11. Draw a square to show a rotation of 90° clockwise about the origin of the given square in quadrant I.

12. What other transformation would result in the same image as you drew in Exercise 11?

    _____

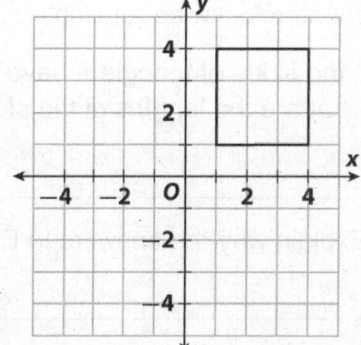

Original content Copyright © by Houghton Mifflin Harcourt. Additions and changes to the original content are the responsibility of the instructor.

Name _____ Date _____ Class _____

LESSON 9-3 Properties of Rotations
Reteach

A **rotation** is a change in position of a figure.

A rotation will *turn* the figure around a point called the **center of rotation**.
A rotation does not change the size of the figure.

At the right, triangle *ABC* has been rotated 90° clockwise. The resulting figure is triangle *A'B'C'*.

Below are two more rotations of triangle *ABC*.

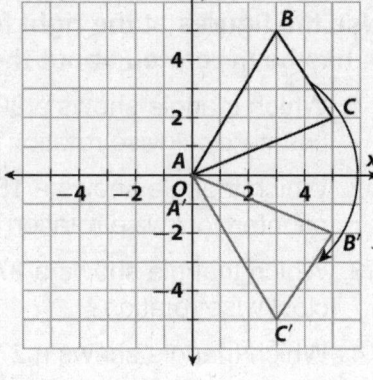

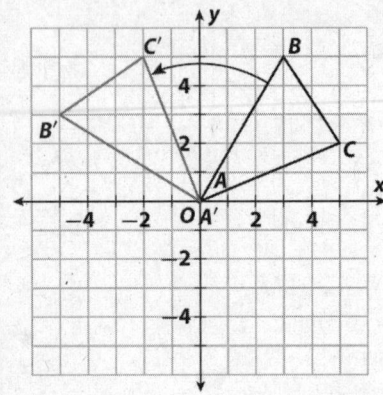
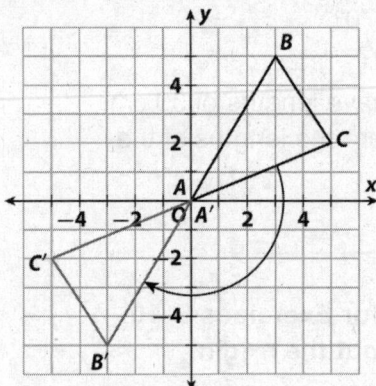

90° counterclockwise rotation   180° clockwise rotation

Use the figures at the right to answer each question. Triangle *A* has been rotated about the origin.

1. Which triangle shows a 90° counterclockwise rotation? ____

2. Which triangle shows a 180° clockwise rotation? ____

3. Which triangle shows a 90° clockwise rotation? ____

4. Which triangle shows a 180° counterclockwise rotation? ____

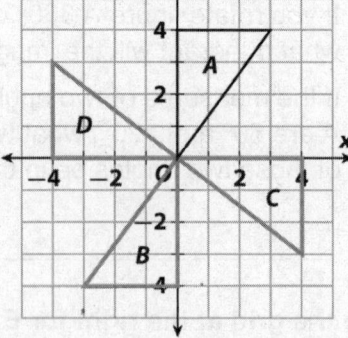

5. If the sides of triangle *A* have lengths of 3 cm, 4 cm, and 5 cm, what are the lengths of the sides of triangle *B*?

_____

6. Explain why the answers to Exercises 2 and 4 are the same.

_____

_____

Name _____ Date _____ Class _____

LESSON 9-4
Algebraic Representations of Transformations
Practice and Problem Solving: A/B

Write an algebraic rule to describe each transformation of figure A to figure A'. Then describe the transformation.

1.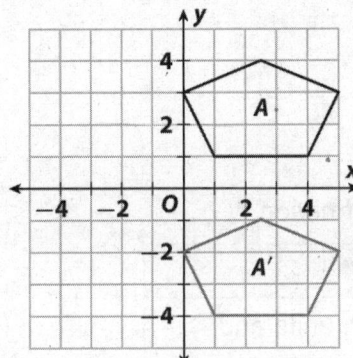

_____

2.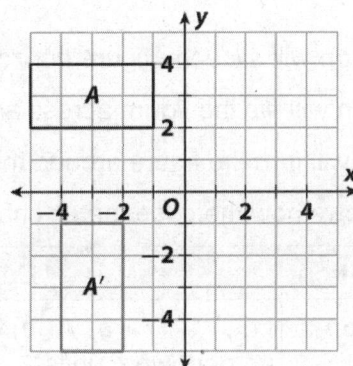

_____

Use the given rule to graph the image of each figure. Then describe the transformation.

3. $(x, y) \to (-x, y)$

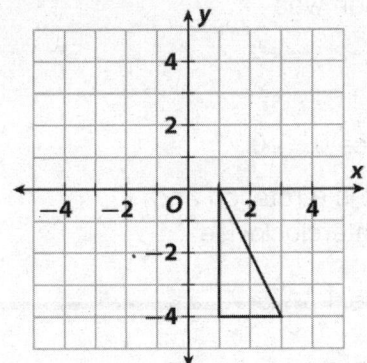

_____

4. $(x, y) \to (-x, -y)$

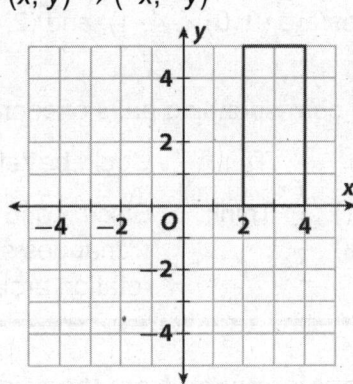

_____

Solve.

5. Triangle ABC has vertices A(2, −1), B(−3, 0), and C(−1, 4). Find the vertices of the image of triangle ABC after a translation of 2 units up.

_____

6. Triangle LMN has L at (1, −1) and M at (2, 3). Triangle L'M'N' has L' at (−1, −1) and M' is at (3, −2). Describe the transformation.

_____

Original content Copyright © by Houghton Mifflin Harcourt. Additions and changes to the original content are the responsibility of the instructor.

Name _____ Date _____ Class _____

LESSON 9-4
Algebraic Representations of Transformations
Reteach

A **transformation** is a change in size or position of a figure. The transformations below change only the position of the figure, not the size.

- A **translation** will *slide* the figure horizontally and/or vertically.
- A **reflection** will *flip* the figure across an axis.
- A **rotation** will *turn* the figure around the origin.

This table shows how the coordinates change with each transformation.

Transformation	Coordinate Mapping
Translation	$(x, y) \rightarrow (x + a, y + b)$ translates left or right a units and up or down b units
Reflection	$(x, y) \rightarrow (-x, y)$ reflects across the y-axis $(x, y) \rightarrow (x, -y)$ reflects across the x-axis
Rotation	$(x, y) \rightarrow (-x, -y)$ rotates 180° around origin $(x, y) \rightarrow (y, -x)$ rotates 90° clockwise around origin $(x, y) \rightarrow (-y, x)$ rotates 90° counterclockwise around origin

A triangle with coordinates of (0, 0), (1, 4), and (3, −2) is transformed so the coordinates are (0, 0), (−4, 1), and (2, 3). What transformation was performed?

Analyze each corresponding pairs of coordinates:

(0, 0) to (0, 0)   Think: Could be reflection or rotation since 0 = −0.

(1, 4) to (−4, 1)   Think: Since x and y are interchanged, it is a rotation and
(3, −2) to (2, 3) y changes sign, so it is a 90° counterclockwise rotation around origin.

Identify the transformation from the original figure to the image.

1. Original: $A(-2, -4)$, $B(5, 1)$, $C(5, -4)$
   Image: $A'(2, -4)$, $B'(-5, 1)$, $C'(-5, -4)$ _____

2. Original: $A(-8, 2)$, $B(-4, 7)$, $C(-7, 2)$
   Image: $A'(-2, -8)$, $B'(-7, -4)$, $C'(-2, -7)$ _____

3. Original: $A(3, 4)$, $B(-1, 2)$, $C(-3, -5)$
   Image: $A'(3, 8)$, $B'(-1, 6)$, $C'(-3, -1)$ _____

4. Original: $A(1, 1)$, $B(2, -2)$, $C(4, 3)$
   Image: $A'(-1, -1)$, $B'(-2, 2)$, $C'(-4, -3)$ _____

5. Original: $A(-5, -6)$, $B(-2, 4)$, $C(3, 0)$
   Image: $A'(-5, 6)$, $B'(-2, -4)$, $C'(3, 0)$ _____

Original content Copyright © by Houghton Mifflin Harcourt. Additions and changes to the original content are the responsibility of the instructor.

Name _____ Date _____ Class _____

LESSON 9-5 Congruent Figures
Practice and Problem Solving: A/B

Identify a sequence of transformations that will transform figure A into figure C.

1. What transformation is used to transform figure *A* to figure *B*?

   _____

2. What transformation is used to transform figure *B* to figure *C*?

   _____

3. What sequence of transformations is used to transform figure *A* to figure *C*? Express the transformations algebraically.

   _____

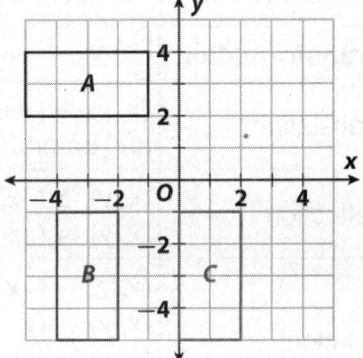

Complete each transformation.

4. Transform figure *A* by reflecting it over the *y*-axis. Label the new figure, *B*.

5. Transform figure *B* to figure *C* by applying $(x, y) \rightarrow (x, y + 5)$.

6. Transform figure *C* to figure *D* by rotating it 90° counterclockwise around the origin.

7. Compare figure *A* with figure *D*. Are the two figures congruent? _____

8. Do figures *A* and *D* have the same or different orientation? _____

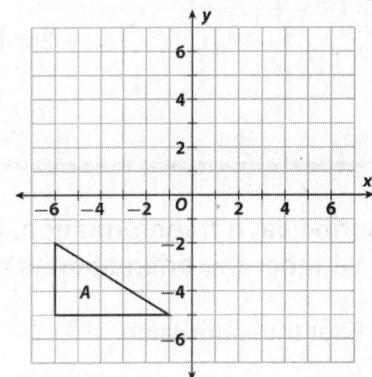

Alice wanted a pool in location A on the map at the right. However, underground wires forced her to move the pool to location B.

9. What transformations were applied to the pool at location *A* to move it to location *B*?

   _____

   _____

10. Did the relocation change the size or orientation of the pool?

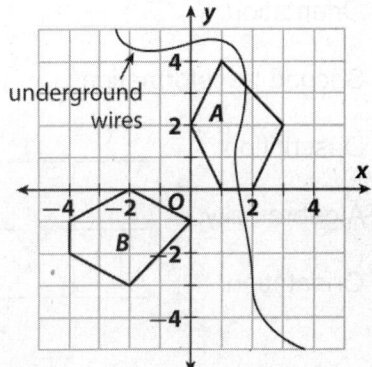

LESSON 9-5 Congruent Figures
Reteach

When combining the transformations below, the original figure and transformed figure are **congruent**. Even though the size does not change, the orientation of the figure might change.

Transformation	Algebraic Coordinate Mapping	Orientation
Translation	$(x, y) \rightarrow (x + a, y + b)$ translates left or right a units and up or down b units	same
Reflection	$(x, y) \rightarrow (-x, y)$ reflects across the y-axis $(x, y) \rightarrow (x, -y)$ reflects across the x-axis	different
Rotation	$(x, y) \rightarrow (-x, -y)$ rotates 180° around origin $(x, y) \rightarrow (y, -x)$ rotates 90° clockwise around origin $(x, y) \rightarrow (-y, x)$ rotates 90° counterclockwise around origin	different

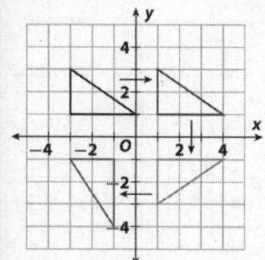

1st transformation: translation right 4 units
$(x, y) \rightarrow (x + 4, y)$, orientation: same

2nd transformation: reflection over the x-axis
$(x, y) \rightarrow (x, -y)$, orientation: different

3rd transformation: rotation 90° clockwise
$(x, y) \rightarrow (y, -x)$ orientation: different

Describe each transformation. Express each algebraically. Tell whether the orientation is the same or different.

1. First transformation

   Description: _____

   Algebraically: _____

   Orientation: _____

2. Second transformation

   Description: _____

   Algebraically: _____

   Orientation: _____

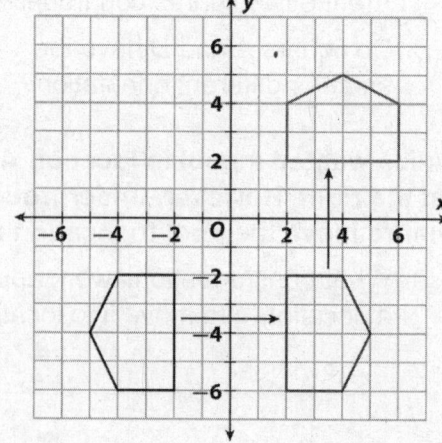

Name _____ Date _____ Class _____

LESSON 10-1
Properties of Dilations
Practice and Problem Solving: A/B

Use triangles ABC and A'B'C' for Exercises 1–4.

1. Use the coordinates to find the lengths of the sides.

   Triangle ABC: AB = ____ ; BC = ____

   Triangle A'B'C': A'B' = ____ ; B'C' = ____

2. Find the ratios of the corresponding sides.

   $\dfrac{A'B'}{AB} = \dfrac{}{} = \underline{}$ $\dfrac{B'C'}{BC} = \dfrac{}{} = \underline{}$

3. Is triangle A'B'C' a dilation of triangle ABC? _____

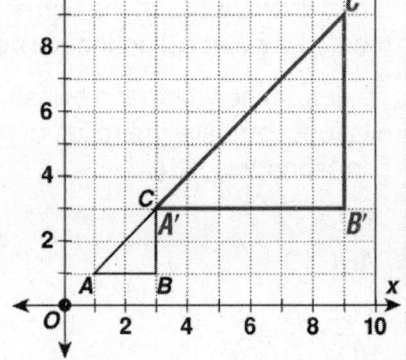

4. If triangle A'B'C' is a dilation of triangle ABC, is it a reduction or an enlargement? _____

For Exercises 5–8, tell whether one figure is a dilation of the other or not. If one figure is a dilation of the other, tell whether it is an enlargement or a reduction. Explain your reasoning.

5. Triangle R'S'T' has sides of 3 cm, 4 cm, and 5 cm. Triangle RST has sides of 12 cm, 16 cm, and 25 cm.

   _____

   _____

6. Quadrilateral WBCD has coordinates of W(0, 0), B(0, 4), C(−6, 4), and D(−6, 0). Quadrilateral W'B'C'D' has coordinates of W'(0, 0), B'(0, 2), C'(−3, 2), and D'(−3, 0).

   _____

   _____

7. Triangle MLQ has sides of 4 cm, 4 cm, and 7 cm. Triangle M'L'Q' has sides of 12 cm, 12 cm, and 21 cm.

   _____

   _____

8. Do the figures at the right show a dilation? Explain.

   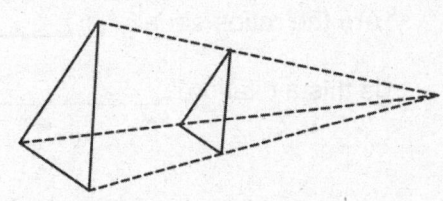

   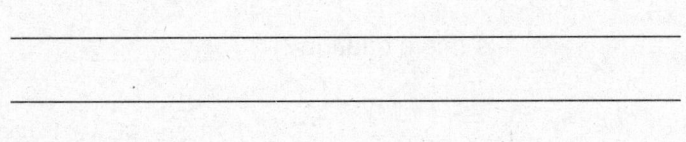

Original content Copyright © by Houghton Mifflin Harcourt. Additions and changes to the original content are the responsibility of the instructor.

Name _____ Date _____ Class _____

LESSON 10-1 Properties of Dilations
Reteach

A **dilation** can change the size of a figure without changing its shape.

Lines drawn through the corresponding vertices meet at a point called the **center of dilation**.

To determine whether a transformation is a dilation, compare the ratios of the lengths of the corresponding sides.

$\dfrac{A'B'}{AB} = \dfrac{2}{1} = 2$

$\dfrac{B'C'}{BC} = \dfrac{6}{3} = 2$

The ratios are equal, so the triangles are similar, and the transformation is a dilation.

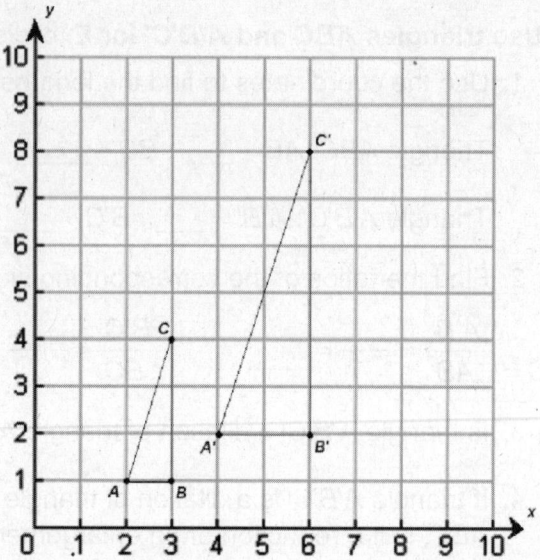

Determine whether each transformation is a dilation.

1.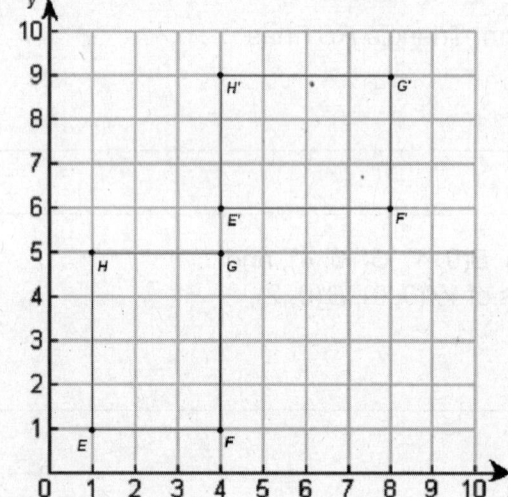

$\dfrac{E'F'}{EF} = \underline{} = \underline{}$

$\dfrac{F'G'}{FG} = \underline{} = \underline{}$

Are the ratios equal? _____

Is this a dilation? _____

2.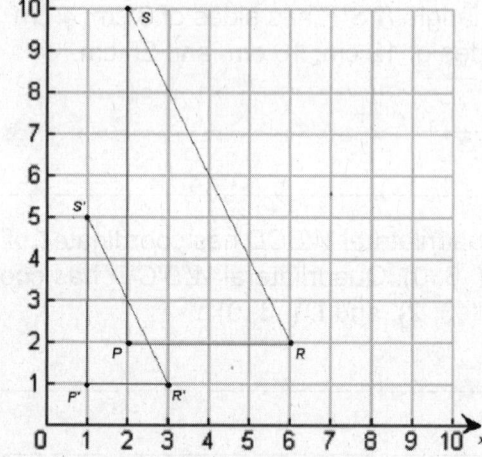

$\dfrac{P'R'}{PR} = \underline{} = \underline{}$

$\dfrac{P'S'}{PS} = \underline{} = \underline{}$

Are the ratios equal? _____

Is this a dilation? _____

Original content Copyright © by Houghton Mifflin Harcourt. Additions and changes to the original content are the responsibility of the instructor.

Name _____ Date _____ Class _____

LESSON 10-2 Algebraic Representations of Dilations
Practice and Problem Solving: A/B

Use triangle ABC for Exercises 1–4.

1. Give the coordinates of each vertex of △ABC.

   A_____ B_____ C_____

2. Multiply each coordinate of the vertices of △ABC by 2 to find the vertices of the dilated image △A'B'C'.

   A'_____ B'_____ C'_____

3. Graph △A'B'C'.

4. Complete this algebraic rule to describe the dilation.

   $(x, y) \rightarrow$ _____

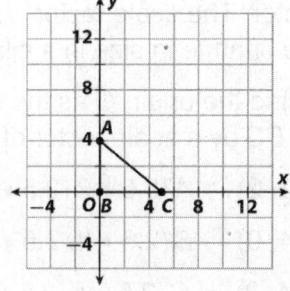

Use the figures at the right for Exercises 5–7.

5. Give the coordinates of each vertex of figure JKLMN.

   J_____ K_____ L_____

   M_____, N_____

6. Give the coordinates of each vertex of figure J'K'L'M'N'.

   J'_____ K'_____ L'_____

   M'_____, N'_____

7. Complete this algebraic rule to describe the dilation.

   $(x, y) \rightarrow$ _____

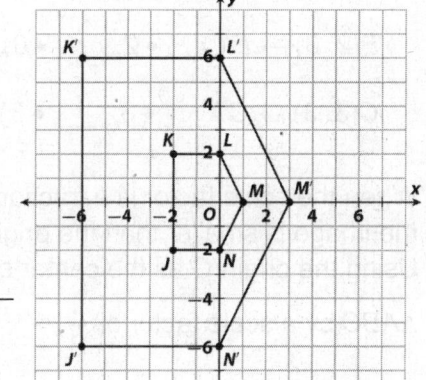

Li made a scale drawing of a room. The scale used was 5 cm = 1 m. The scale drawing is the preimage and the room is the dilated image.

8. What is the scale in terms of centimeters to centimeters?

   _____

9. Complete this algebraic rule to describe the dilation from the scale drawing to the room.

   $(x, y) \rightarrow$ _____

10. The scale drawing measures 15 centimeters by 20 centimeters. What are the dimensions of the room?

    _____

Original content Copyright © by Houghton Mifflin Harcourt. Additions and changes to the original content are the responsibility of the instructor.

Name _____ Date _____ Class _____

LESSON 10-2
Algebraic Representations of Dilations
Reteach

You dilate a figure using the origin as the center of dilation. Multiply each coordinate by the scale factor. The scale factor is the number that describes the change in size in a dilation.

Using the origin O as the center of dilation, dilate △ABC by a scale factor of 2.5.

$A(2, 2) \rightarrow A'(2.5 \cdot 2, 2.5 \cdot 2)$ or $A'(5, 5)$

$B(4, 0) \rightarrow B'(2.5 \cdot 4, 2.5 \cdot 0)$ or $B'(10, 0)$

$C(4, 2) \rightarrow C'(2.5 \cdot 4, 2.5 \cdot 2)$ or $C'(10, 5)$

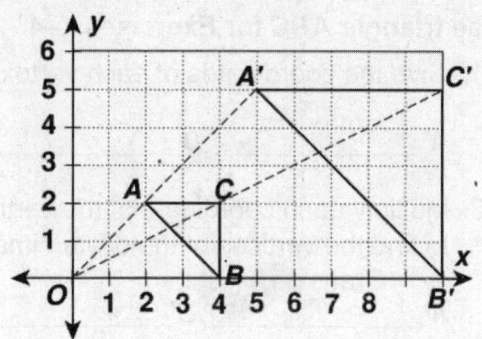

Using the origin as the center of dilation, dilate △ABC by a scale factor of 2. Graph the dilation.

1. $A(1, 2) \rightarrow A'(2 \cdot 1, 2 \cdot 2)$ or $A'(\_\_\_, \_\_\_)$

   $B(2, 0) \rightarrow B'(\_\_\_ \cdot 2, \_\_\_ \cdot 0)$ or $B'(\_\_\_, \_\_\_)$

   $C(3, 3) \rightarrow C'(\_\_\_ \cdot 3, \_\_\_ \cdot 3)$ or $C'(\_\_\_, \_\_\_)$

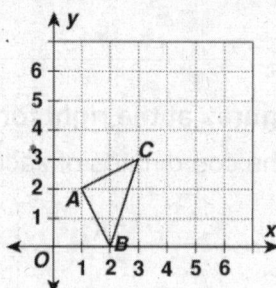

When the scale factor is a fraction between 0 and 1, the image is smaller than the original figure.
Using the origin O as the center of dilation, dilate △ABC by a scale factor of $\frac{1}{3}$.

$A(3, 3) \rightarrow A'\left(\frac{1}{3} \cdot 3, \frac{1}{3} \cdot 3\right)$ or $A'(1, 1)$

$B(6, 0) \rightarrow B'\left(\frac{1}{3} \cdot 6, \frac{1}{3} \cdot 0\right)$ or $B'(2, 0)$

$C(6, 6) \rightarrow C'\left(\frac{1}{3} \cdot 6, \frac{1}{3} \cdot 6\right)$ or $C'(2, 2)$

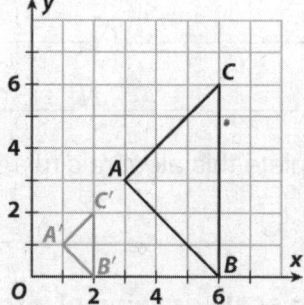

Using the origin as the center of dilation, dilate △ABC by a scale factor of $\frac{1}{2}$. Graph the dilation.

2. $A(8, 0) \rightarrow A'\left(\frac{1}{2} \cdot 8, \frac{1}{2} \cdot 0\right)$ or $A'(\_\_\_, \_\_\_)$

   $B(4, 4) \rightarrow B'(\_\_\_ \cdot 4, \_\_\_ \cdot 4)$ or $B'(\_\_\_, \_\_\_)$

   $C(6, 8) \rightarrow C'(\_\_\_ \cdot 6, \_\_\_ \cdot 8)$ or $C'(\_\_\_, \_\_\_)$

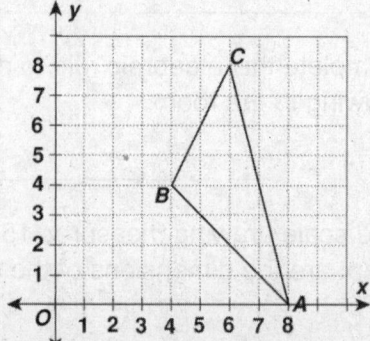

Original content Copyright © by Houghton Mifflin Harcourt. Additions and changes to the original content are the responsibility of the instructor.

Name _____ Date _____ Class_____

LESSON 10-3
Similar Figures
Practice and Problem Solving: A/B

Identify a sequence of transformations that will transform figure A into figure C. Express each transformation algebraically.

1. What transformation is used to transform figure A to figure B?
   _____

2. What transformation is used to transform figure B to figure C?
   _____

— Figure A
— Figure B
- - Figure C

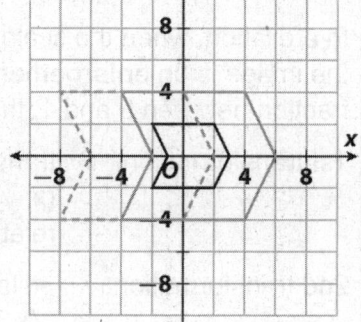

3. Name two figures that are congruent. _____

4. Name two figures that are similar, but not congruent. _____

Complete each transformation.

5. Transform figure A to figure B by applying $(x, y) \to (2x, 2y)$.

6. Transform figure B to figure C by rotating it 90° clockwise around the origin.

7. Name two figures that are congruent.
   _____

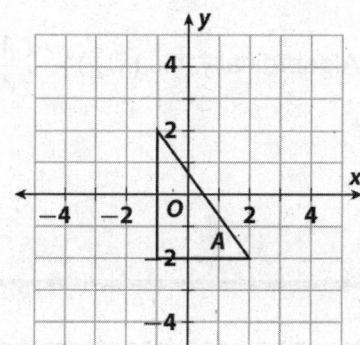

8. Name two figures that are similar, but not congruent.
   _____

Geraldo designed a flag for his school. He started with △ABC. He used centimeter grid paper. To create the actual flag, the drawing must be dilated using a scale factor of 50. Express each transformation algebraically.

9. What transformation was used to create △CBD from △ABC?
   _____

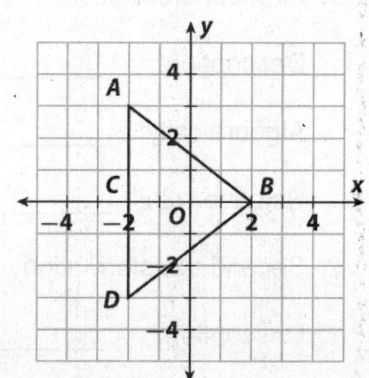

10. How long will each side of the actual flag ABD be?
    _____

11. The principal decides he wants the flag to hang vertically with side AD on top. What transformation should Geraldo use on △ABD on his drawing so it is in the desired orientation?
    _____

Original content Copyright © by Houghton Mifflin Harcourt. Additions and changes to the original content are the responsibility of the instructor.

Name _____ Date _____ Class _____

LESSON 10-3 Similar Figures
Reteach

Multiple dilations can be applied to a figure. If one of the transformations is a **dilation**, the figure and its image are **similar**. The size of the figure is changed but the shape is not.

In a dilation, when the scale is a greater than 1, the image is an **enlargement**. When the scale is a fraction between 0 and 1, the image is a **reduction**.

1st transformation: translation right 6 units
$(x, y) \rightarrow (x + 6, y)$,
relative size: congruent

2nd transformation: dilation by a scale of 3
$(x, y) \rightarrow (3x, 3y)$
relative size: similar

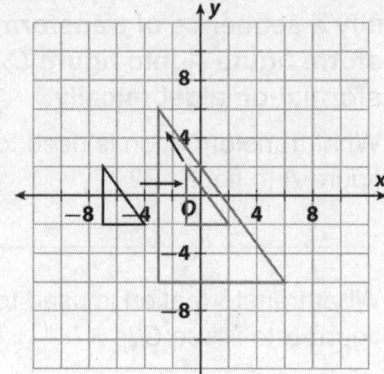

The dilation at the right has a scale of $\frac{1}{4}$.

Algebraically it is $(x, y) \rightarrow \left(\frac{1}{4}x, \frac{1}{4}y\right)$

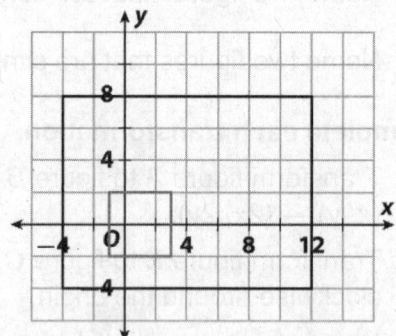

Describe each transformation. Express each one algebraically. Tell whether the figure and its image are congruent or are similar.

1. First transformation:

   Description: _____

   Algebraically: _____

   Relative size: _____

2. Second transformation:

   Description: _____

   Algebraically: _____

   Relative size: _____

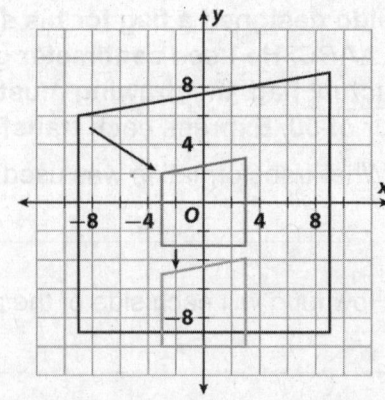

Name _____ Date _____ Class _____

LESSON 11-1
Parallel Lines Cut by a Transversal
Practice and Problem Solving: A/B

Use the figure at the right for Exercises 1–6.

1. Name both pairs of alternate interior angles.

   _____

2. Name the corresponding angle to ∠3. ___

3. Name the relationship between ∠1 and ∠5.

   _____

4. Name the relationship between ∠2 and ∠3.

   _____

5. Name an interior angle that is supplementary to ∠7. _____

6. Name an exterior angle that is supplementary to ∠5. _____

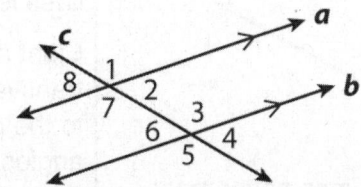

Use the figure at the right for problems 7–10. Line *MP* ∥ line *QS*. Find the angle measures.

7. m∠KRQ when m∠KNM = 146° ___

8. m∠QRN when m∠MNR = 52° ___

If m∠RNP = (8x + 63)° and m∠NRS = 5x°, find the following angle measures.

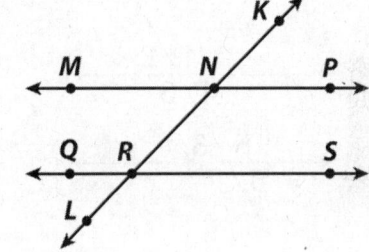

9. m∠RNP = _____   10. m∠NRS = _____

In the figure at the right, there are no parallel lines. Use the figure for problems 11–14.

11. Name both pairs of alternate exterior angles.

    _____

12. Name the corresponding angle to ∠4 ___

13. Name the relationship between ∠3 and ∠6.

    _____

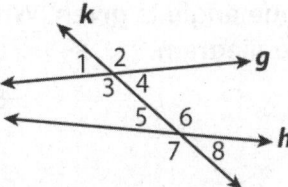

14. Are there any supplementary angles? If so, name two pairs. If not, explain why not.

    _____

Original content Copyright © by Houghton Mifflin Harcourt. Additions and changes to the original content are the responsibility of the instructor.

Name _____ Date _____ Class _____

LESSON 11-1 Parallel Lines Cut by a Transversal
Reteach

Parallel Lines

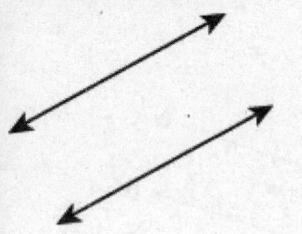

Parallel lines never meet.

Parallel Lines Cut by a Transversal

A line that crosses parallel lines is a **transversal**.

Eight angles are formed. If the transversal is not perpendicular to the parallel lines, then four angles are acute and four are obtuse.

The acute angles are all congruent.

The obtuse angles are all congruent.

Any acute angle is supplementary to any obtuse angle.

In each diagram, parallel lines are cut by a transversal. Name the angles that are congruent to the indicated angle.

1.

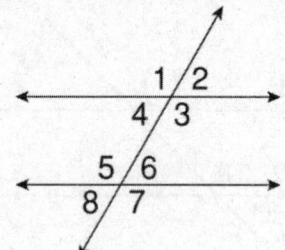

The angles congruent to ∠1 are: _____

2.

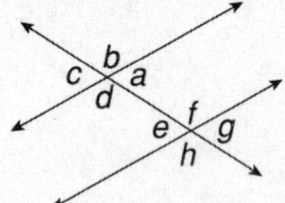

The angles congruent to ∠a are: _____

3.

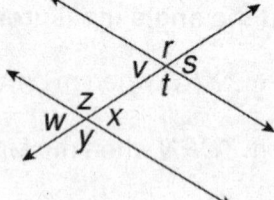

The angles congruent to ∠z are: _____

In each diagram, parallel lines are cut by a transversal and the measure of one angle is given. Write the measures of the remaining angles on the diagram.

4.

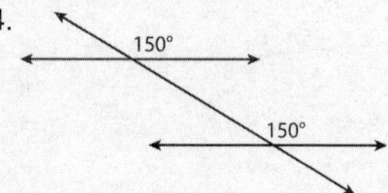

5.

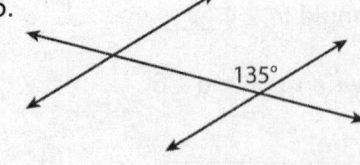

6.

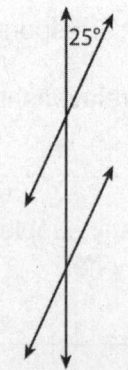

Name _____ Date _____ Class _____

LESSON 11-2 Angle Theorems for Triangles
Practice and Problem Solving: A/B

Find the measure of each unknown angle.

1.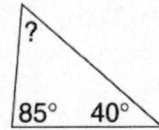

2.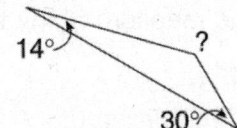

3.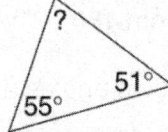

_____ _____ _____

4.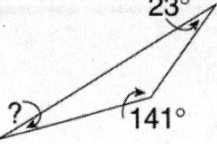

5.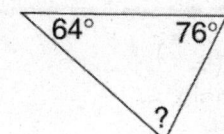

6.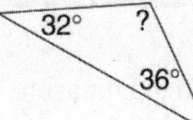

_____ _____ _____

7.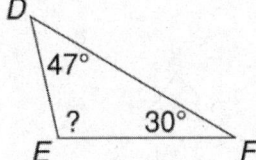

8.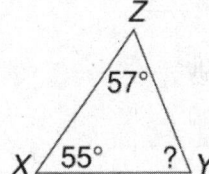

9.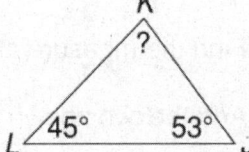

_____ _____ _____

Use the diagram at the right to answer each question below.

10. What is the measure of ∠DEF?

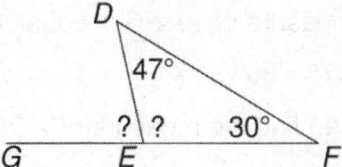

_____

11. What is the measure of ∠DEG?

_____

12. A triangular sign has three angles that all have the same measure. What is the measure of each angle?

_____

LESSON 11-2

Angle Theorems for Triangles
Reteach

If you know the measure of two angles in a triangle, you can subtract their sum from 180°. The difference is the measure of the third angle.

The two known angles are 60° and 55°.

$60° + 55° = 115°$

$180° - 115° = 65°$

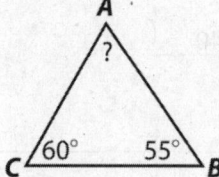

Solve.

1. Find the measure of the unknown angle.

   Add the two known angles: ___ + ___ = ___

   Subtract the sum from 180°: 180 – ___ = ___

   The measure of the unknown angle is: ___

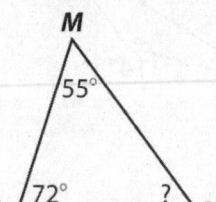

2. Find the measure of the unknown angle.

   Add the two known angles: ___ + ___ = ___

   Subtract the sum from 180°: 180 – ___ = ___

   The measure of the unknown angle is: ___

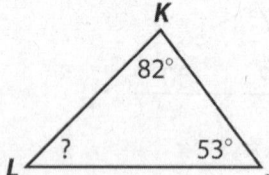

∠DEG is an **exterior angle**.

The measure of ∠DEG is equal to the sum of ∠D and ∠F.

$47° + 30° = 77°$

You can find the measure of ∠DEF by subtracting 77° from 180°.

$180° - 77° = 103°$

The measure of ∠DEF is 103°.

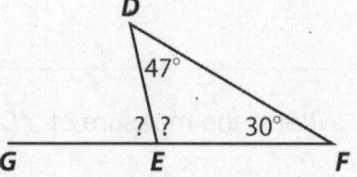

Solve.

3. Find the measure of angle y.

   85° + 65° = _____

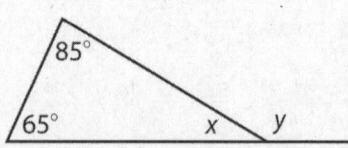

4. Find the measure of angle x.

   180° – ___ = ___

Name _____ Date _____ Class _____

LESSON 11-3 Angle-Angle Similarity
Practice and Problem Solving: A/B

Explain whether the triangles are similar.

1.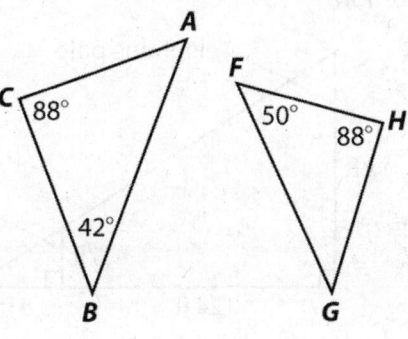

2.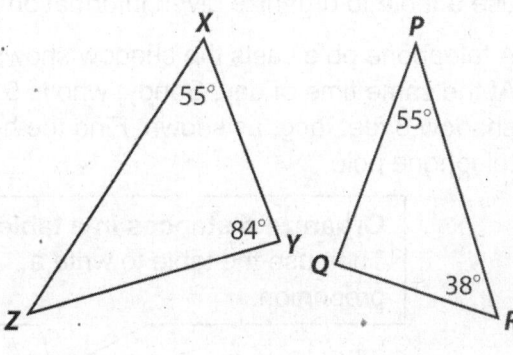

_____   _____
_____   _____
_____   _____

The diagram below shows a Howe roof truss, which is used to frame the roof of a building. Use it to answer problems 3–5.

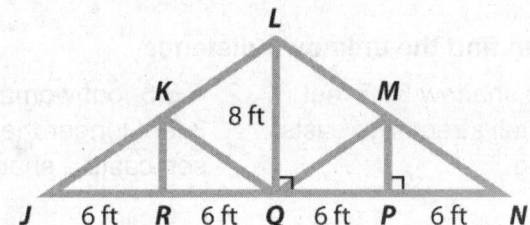

3. Explain why △LQN is similar to △MPN.

   _____

4. What is the length of support MP? _____

5. Using the information in the diagram, can you determine whether △LQJ is similar to △KRJ? Explain.

   _____

6. In the diagram at the right, sides SV and RW are parallel.
   Explain why △RTW is similar to △STV.

   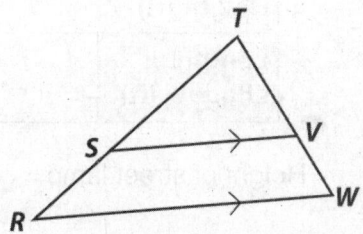

   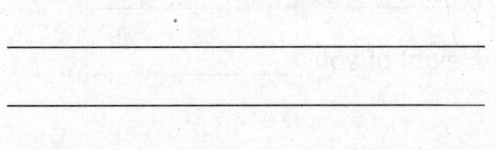

Original content Copyright © by Houghton Mifflin Harcourt. Additions and changes to the original content are the responsibility of the instructor.

LESSON 11-3 Angle-Angle Similarity
Reteach

When solving triangle similarity problems involving proportions, you can use a table to organize given information and set up a proportion.

A telephone pole casts the shadow shown on the diagram. At the same time of day, Sandy, who is 5 feet tall, casts a shadow 8 feet long, as shown. Find the height of the telephone pole.

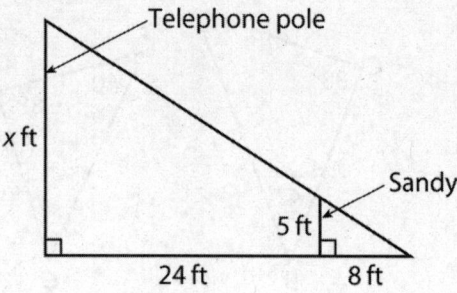

Organize distances in a table. Then use the table to write a proportion.

	Pole	Sandy
Height (ft)	x	5
Length of shadow (ft)	24 + 8, or 32	8

$$\frac{x}{32} = \frac{5}{8}$$

Solve the proportion. The height of the telephone pole is 20 feet.

Complete the table. Then find the unknown distance.

1. A street lamp casts a shadow 31.5 feet long, while an 8-foot tall street sign casts a shadow 14 feet long.

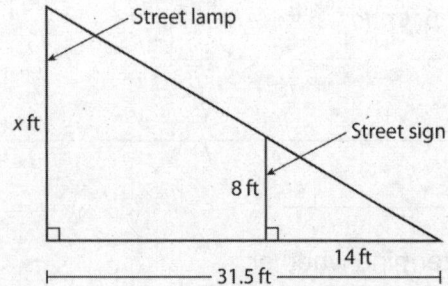

	Lamp	Sign
Height (ft)		
Length of shadow (ft)		

Height of street lamp = _____

2. A 5.5-foot woman casts a shadow that is 3 feet longer than her son's shadow. The son casts a shadow 13.5 feet long.

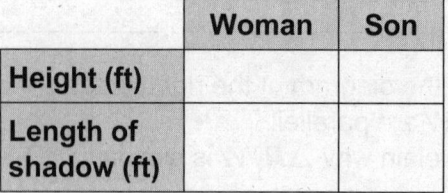

	Woman	Son
Height (ft)		
Length of shadow (ft)		

Height of son = _____

Name _____ Date _____ Class _____

LESSON 12-1 The Pythagorean Theorem
Practice and Problem Solving: A/B

Find the missing side to the nearest tenth.

1.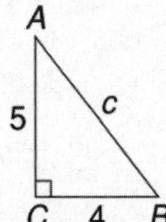

2.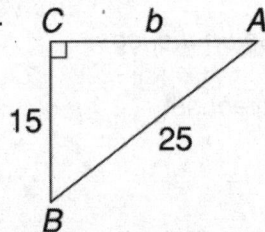

3.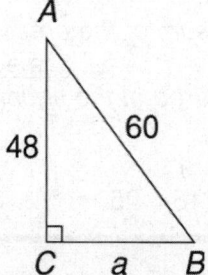

_____   _____   _____

4.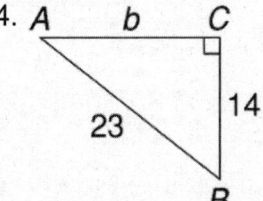

5.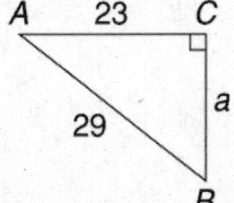

6.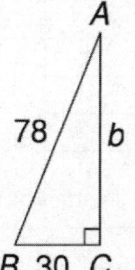

_____   _____   _____

Solve.

7. Jane and Miguel are siblings. They go to different schools. Jane walks 6 blocks east from home. Miguel walks 8 blocks north. How many blocks apart would the two schools be if you could walk straight from one school to the other?

_____

8. The base of a rectangular box has a width of 3 inches and a length of 4 inches. The box is 12 inches tall.

   a. Draw a picture of the box below.

   b. How far is it from one of the box's top corners to the opposite corner of the base of the box?

_____

Original content Copyright © by Houghton Mifflin Harcourt. Additions and changes to the original content are the responsibility of the instructor.

Name _____ Date _____ Class _____

LESSON 12-1
The Pythagorean Theorem
Reteach

In a **right triangle**,

the sum of the areas of the squares on the legs
is equal to
the area of the square on the hypotenuse.

$3^2 + 4^2 = 5^2$
$9 + 16 = 25$

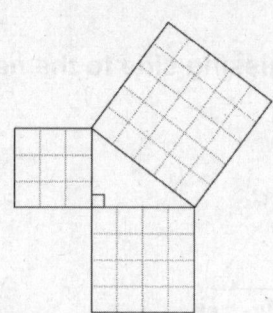

Given the squares that are on the legs of a right triangle, draw the square for the hypotenuse below or on another sheet of paper.

1. leg   leg   hypotenuse

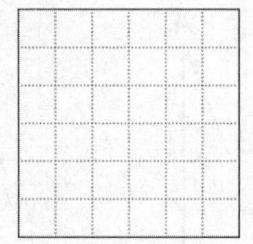 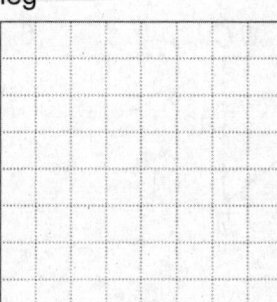

Without drawing the squares, you can find a missing leg or the hypotenuse when given the other sides.

Model   **Example 1**   **Example 2**

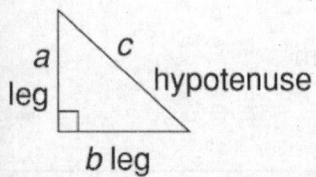 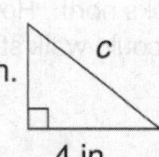 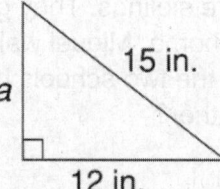

                     Solution 1   **Solution 2**
                     $a^2 + b^2 = c^2$ $a^2 + b^2 = c^2$
                     $3^2 + 4^2 = c^2$ $a^2 + 12^2 = 15^2$
                     $9 + 16 = c^2$ $a^2 = 225 - 144$
                     $25 = c^2$, so $c = 5$ in. $a^2 = 81$, so $a = 9$ in.

Find the missing side.

2.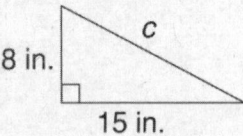

3.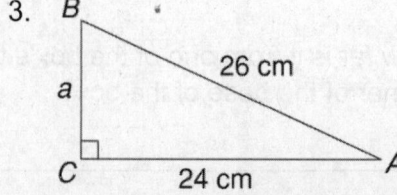

LESSON 12-2 Converse of the Pythagorean Theorem
Practice and Problem Solving: A/B

Write "yes" for sides that form right triangles and "no" for sides that do not form right triangles. Prove that each answer is correct.

1. 7, 24, 25

2. 30, 40, 45

3. 21.6, 28.8, 36

4. 10, 15, 18

5. 10.5, 36, 50

6. 2.5, 6, 6.5

Solve.

7. A commuter airline files a new route between two cities that are 400 kilometers apart. One of the two cities is 200 kilometers from a third city. The other one of the two cities is 300 kilometers from the third city. Do the paths between the three cities form a right triangle? Prove that your answer is correct.

8. A school wants to build a rectangular playground that will have a diagonal length of 75 yards. How wide can the playground be if the length has to be 30 yards?

9. A 250-foot length of fence is placed around a three-sided animal pen. Two of the sides of the pen are 100 feet long each. Does the fence form a right triangle? Prove that your answer is correct.

Name _____ Date _____ Class _____

LESSON 12-2

Converse of the Pythagorean Theorem
Reteach

Step 1 The first step in verifying that a triangle is a right triangle is to name the three sides. One side is the hypotenuse and the other two sides are legs.

- In a right triangle, the hypotenuse is opposite the right angle.

  → The hypotenuse is 5 cm.

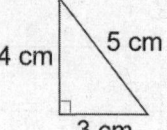

- The hypotenuse is greater than either leg.

  → 5 cm > 4 cm and 5 cm > 3 cm

Step 2 Next, the lengths of the hypotenuse and legs must satisfy the Pythagorean Theorem.

$$(\text{hypotenuse})^2 = (\text{first leg})^2 + (\text{second leg})^2$$

In the example above, $5^2 = 3^2 + 4^2 = 25$, so the triangle is a right triangle.

Conclusion If the lengths of the hypotenuse and the two legs satisfy the conditions of the Pythagorean Theorem, then the triangle is a right triangle. If they do not satisfy the conditions of the Pythagorean Theorem, the triangle is not a right triangle.

Find the length of each hypotenuse.

1.

2.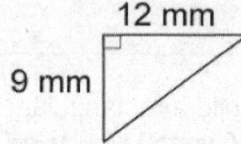

_____   _____

First, fill in the length of the hypotenuse in each problem. Then, determine if the sides form a right triangle.

3. 1, 2, 3

   Hypotenuse: _____

   _____

4. 8, 7, 6

   Hypotenuse: _____

   _____

5. 15, 20, 25

   Hypotenuse: _____

   _____

Show that these sides form a right triangle.

6. 2, 3, $\sqrt{13}$

   _____

7. 3, 6, $3\sqrt{5}$

   _____

Name _____ Date _____ Class _____

LESSON 12-3 Distance Between Two Points
Practice and Problem Solving: A/B

Name the coordinates of the points.

1.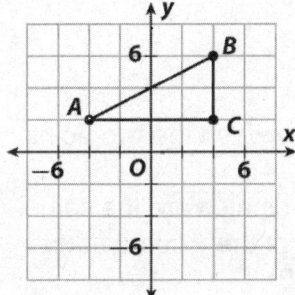

2.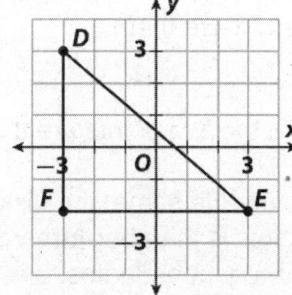

A(_____ , _____)

B(_____ , _____)

C(_____ , _____)

D(_____ , _____)

E(_____ , _____)

F(_____ , _____)

Name the hypotenuse of each right triangle in problems 1 and 2.

3. Hypotenuse in problem 1:
_____

4. Hypotenuse in problem 2:
_____

Estimate the length of the hypotenuse for each right triangle in problems 1 and 2.

5. Hypotenuse in problem 1:
_____

6. Hypotenuse in problem 2:
_____

Use the distance formula to calculate the length of the hypotenuse for each right triangle.

7. Hypotenuse in problem 1:
_____
_____

8. Hypotenuse in problem 2:
_____
_____

9. Use the distance formula to find the distance between the points (−4, −4) and (4, 4).

_____

LESSON 12-3 Distance Between Two Points
Reteach

There are three cases of distance between two points on a coordinate plane. The first two have fewer steps than the third, but you have to be able to identify when to use them.

Case 1
The x-coordinates of the two points are the same.
If the x-coordinates are the same, the distance between the two points is the **absolute value** of the *difference* of the y-coordinates.
The line connecting the two points is a *vertical* line.

Example 1
Find the distance between the two points $A(-3, 5)$ and $B(-3, -4)$.
⟶ The x-coordinates are the same.
⟶ Difference of the y-coordinates:
  $5 - (-4) = 9$
⟶ The absolute value of 9 is 9.

Case 2
The y-coordinates of the two points are the same.
If the y-coordinates are the same, the distance between the two points is the **absolute value** of the *difference* of the x-coordinates.
The line connecting the two points is a *horizontal* line.

Example 2
Find the distance between the two points $C(1, 3)$ and $D(6, 3)$.
⟶ The y-coordinates are the same.
⟶ Difference of the x-coordinates:
  $1 - 6 = -5$
⟶ The absolute value of -5 is 5.

Case 3
If the x and y-coordinates of the two points are different, use the distance formula:
$d = \sqrt{(x_2 - x_1)^2 + (y_2 - y_1)^2}$
The x and y-coordinates are different if $x_1 \neq x_2$ and $y_1 \neq y_2$.
The line connecting the two points can be thought of as the *hypotenuse* of a right triangle.

Example 3
Find the distance between the two points $E(-9, 5)$ and $F(-4, 0)$.
⟶ Use the distance formula.
⟶ $d = \sqrt{(-4+9)^2 + (0-5)^2}$
  $= \sqrt{5^2 + (-5)^2} = 5\sqrt{2}$

Tell whether the points given are endpoints of a vertical line, a horizontal line, or neither.

1. $(-8, 1), (-5, 1)$
2. $(4, 3), (2, 1)$
3. $(0, 0), (0, 100)$
4. $(3, 3), (3, 3)$

Use the distance formula to find the distance between the two points.

5. $(0.5, 1.3), (-0.4, -1.2)$
6. $(6, -3), (2, -4)$

Name _____ Date _____ Class _____

LESSON 13-1 Volume of Cylinders
Practice and Problem Solving: A/B

Find the volume of each cylinder. Round your answer to the nearest tenth if necessary. Use 3.14 for π.

1. 6.5 cm
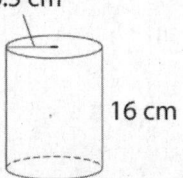
16 cm

_____

2. 4 in.
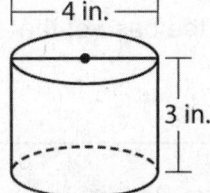
3 in.

_____

3. A cylindrical oil drum has a diameter of 2 feet and a height of 3 feet. What is the volume of the oil drum?

   _____

4. New Oats cereal is packaged in a cardboard cylinder. The packaging is 10 inches tall with a diameter of 3 inches. What is the volume of the New Oats cereal package?

   _____

5. A small plastic storage container is in the shape of a cylinder. It has a diameter of 7.6 centimeters and a height of 3 centimeters. What is the volume of the storage cylinder?

   _____

6. A can of juice has a diameter of 6.6 centimeters and a height of 12.1 centimeters. What is the total volume of a six-pack of juice cans?

   _____

7. Mr. Macady has an old cylindrical grain silo on his farm that stands 25 feet high with a diameter of 10 feet. Mr. Macady is planning to tear down the old silo and replace it with a new and bigger one. The new cylindrical silo will stand 30 feet high and have a diameter of 15 feet.

   a. What is the volume of the old silo? _____

   b. What is the volume of the new silo? _____

   c. How much greater is the volume of the new silo than the old silo?

   _____

Name _____ Date _____ Class _____

LESSON 13-1 Volume of Cylinders
Reteach

You can use your knowledge of how to find the area of a circle to find the volume of a cylinder.

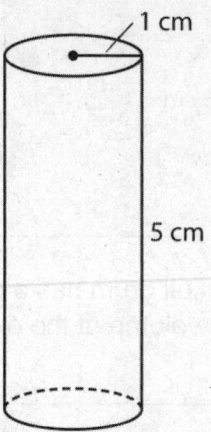

1. What is the shape of the base of the cylinder?

   _____ circle _____

2. The area of the base is $B = \pi r^2$.

   $B = 3.14 \cdot \underline{\;1\;}^2 = \underline{3.14}$ cm²

3. The height of the cylinder is __5__ cm.

4. The volume of the cylinder is

   $V = B \cdot h = \underline{3.14} \cdot \underline{\;5\;} = \underline{15.7}$ cm³

The volume of the cylinder is 15.7 cm³.

---

1. a. What is the area of the base?

      $B = 3.14 \cdot \underline{\quad}^2 = \underline{\quad}$ cm²

   b. What is the height of the cylinder? ____ cm

   c. What is the volume of the cylinder?

      $V = B \cdot h = \underline{\quad} \cdot \underline{\quad} = \underline{\quad}$ cm³

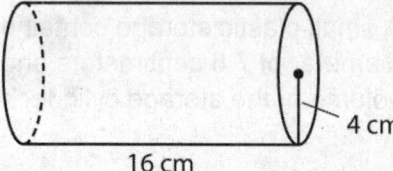

2. a. What is the area of the base?

      $B = 3.14 \cdot \underline{\quad}^2 = \underline{\quad}$ cm²

   b. What is the height of the cylinder? ____ cm

   c. What is the volume of the cylinder?

      $V = B \cdot h = \underline{\quad} \cdot \underline{\quad} = \underline{\quad}$ cm³

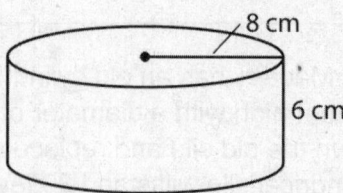

Original content Copyright © by Houghton Mifflin Harcourt. Additions and changes to the original content are the responsibility of the instructor.

Name _____ Date _____ Class _____

LESSON 13-2 Volume of Cones
Practice and Problem Solving: A/B

Find the volume of each cone. Round your answer to the nearest tenth if necessary. Use 3.14 for π.

1.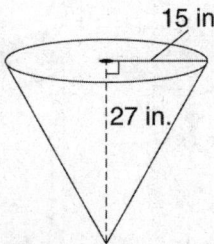

   15 in.
   27 in.

   _____

2.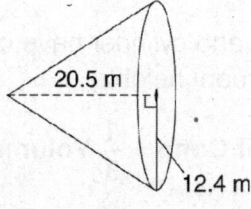

   20.5 m
   12.4 m

   _____

3. The mold for a cone has a diameter of 4 inches and is 6 inches tall. What is the volume of the cone mold to the nearest tenth?

   _____

4. A medium-sized paper cone has a diameter of 8 centimeters and a height of 10 centimeters. What is the volume of the cone?

   _____

5. A funnel has a diameter of 9 in. and is 16 in. tall. A plug is put at the open end of the funnel. What is the volume of the cone to the nearest tenth?

   _____

6. A party hat has a diameter of 10 cm and is 15 cm tall. What is the volume of the hat?

   _____

7. Find the volume of the composite figure to the nearest tenth. Use 3.14 for π.

   a. Volume of cone:

      _____

   b. Volume of cylinder:

      _____

   c. Volume of composite figure:

      _____

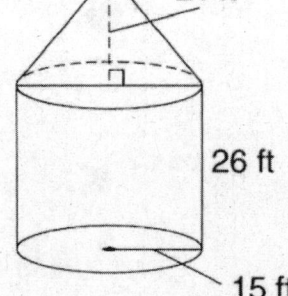

21 ft
26 ft
15 ft

Name _____ Date _____ Class _____

LESSON 13-2 Volume of Cones
Reteach

You can use your knowledge of how to find the volume of a cylinder to help find the volume of a cone.

This cone and cylinder have congruent bases and congruent heights.

Volume of Cone = $\frac{1}{3}$ Volume of Cylinder

Use this formula to find the volume of a cone.

$$V = \frac{1}{3}Bh$$

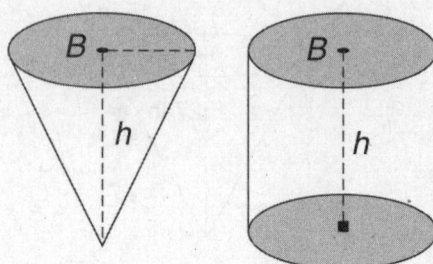

Complete to find the volume of each cone.

1.

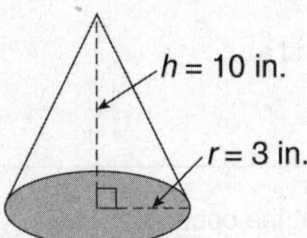

radius r of base = ____ in.

$V = \frac{1}{3}Bh$

$V = \frac{1}{3}(\pi r^2)h$

$V = \frac{1}{3}(\pi \times \underline{}) \times \underline{}$

$V = \frac{1}{3}(\underline{}) \times \underline{}$

$V = \underline{} \times \underline{}$

$V = \underline{}$

$V \approx \underline{}$ in^3

2.

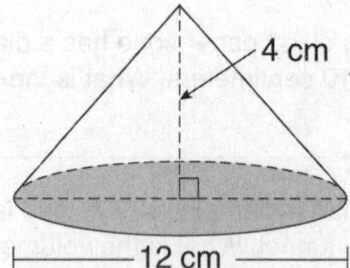

radius $r = \frac{1}{2}$ diameter = ____ cm

$V = \frac{1}{3}Bh$

$V = \frac{1}{3}(\pi r^2)h$

$V = \frac{1}{3}(\pi \times \underline{}) \times \underline{}$

$V = \frac{1}{3}(\underline{}) \times \underline{}$

$V = \underline{} \times \underline{}$

$V = \underline{}$

$V \approx \underline{}$ cm^3

Name _____ Date _____ Class _____

LESSON 13-3 Volume of Spheres
Practice and Problem Solving: A/B

Find the volume of each sphere. Round your answer to the nearest tenth if necessary. $V = \frac{4}{3}\pi r^3$. Use 3.14 for π. Show your work.

1.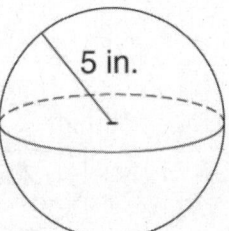

2.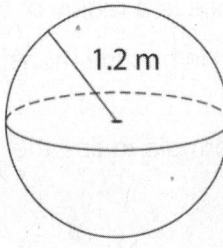

3. $r = 3$ inches   4. $d = 9$ feet   5. $r = 1.5$ meters

_____   _____   _____

6. A globe is a map of Earth shaped as a sphere. What is the volume, to the nearest tenth, of a globe with a diameter of 16 inches?

_____

7. The maximum diameter of a bowling ball is 8.6 inches. What is the volume to the nearest tenth of a bowling ball with this diameter?

_____

8. According to the National Collegiate Athletic Association men's rules, a tennis ball must have a diameter of more than $2\frac{1}{2}$ inches and less than $2\frac{5}{8}$ inches.

   a. What is the volume of a sphere with a diameter of $2\frac{1}{2}$ inches?

   _____

   b. What is the volume of a sphere with a diameter of $2\frac{5}{8}$ inches?

   _____

   c. Write an inequality that expresses the range in the volume of acceptable tennis balls.

   _____

Original content Copyright © by Houghton Mifflin Harcourt. Additions and changes to the original content are the responsibility of the instructor.

Name _____ Date _____ Class _____

LESSON 13-3 Volume of Spheres
Reteach

- All points on a sphere are the same distance from its center.
- Any line drawn from the center of a sphere to its surface is a radius of the sphere.
- The radius is half the measure of the diameter.
- Use this formula to find the volume of a sphere.

$$V = \frac{4}{3}\pi r^3$$

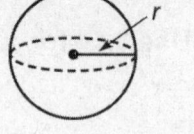
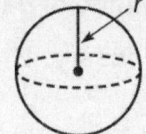
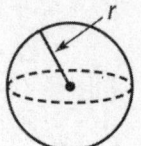
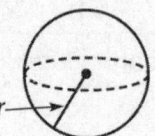

Complete to find the volume of each sphere to the nearest tenth. Use 3.14 for π. The first one is done for you.

1. A regular tennis ball has a diameter of 2.5 inches.

    diameter = __2.5 inches__

    radius = __1.25 inches__

    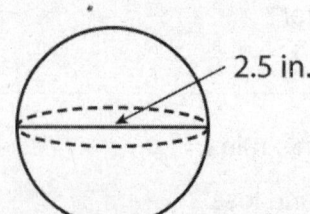

    $V = \frac{4}{3}\pi r^3$

    $V = \frac{4}{3} \cdot \underline{3.14} \cdot \underline{1.25^3}$

    $V = \frac{4}{3} \cdot \underline{3.14} \cdot \underline{1.95}$

    $V = \underline{8.164}$

    $V \approx \underline{8.2 \text{ in}^3}$

2. A large grapefruit has a diameter of 12 centimeters.

    diameter = _____

    radius = _____

    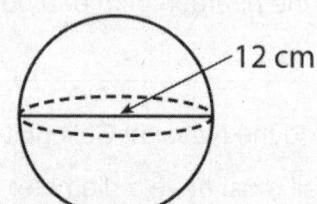

    $V = \frac{4}{3}\pi r^3$

    $V = \frac{4}{3} \cdot \underline{} \cdot \underline{}$

    $V = \frac{4}{3} \cdot \underline{} \cdot \underline{}$

    $V = \underline{}$

    $V \approx \underline{}$

Name _____ Date _____ Class _____

LESSON 14-1 Scatter Plots and Association
Practice and Problem Solving: A/B

1. Use the given data to make a scatter plot.

Calories and Fat Per Portion of Meat and Fish

Food (Meat or Fish)	Fat (grams)	Calories
Fish Sticks (breaded)	3	50
Shrimp (fried)	9	190
Tuna (canned in oil)	7	170
Ground beef (broiled)	10	185
Roast beef (relatively lean)	7	165
Ham (light cure, lean and fat)	19	245

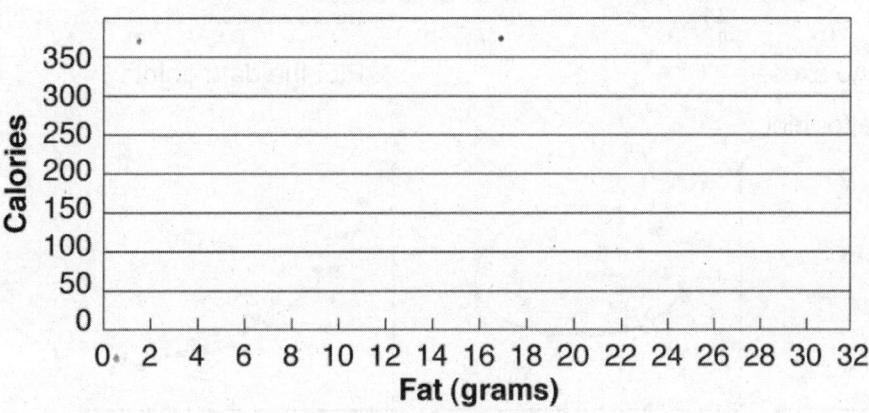

Calories and Fat Per Portion of Meat and Fish

Do the data sets have a positive, a negative, or no correlation?

2. The size of the bag of popcorn and the price of popcorn

   _____

3. The temperature and number of snowboards sold

   _____

4. Use the data to predict how much money Tyler would be paid for babysitting $7\frac{1}{2}$ hours.

Amount Tyler Earns Babysitting

Hours	1	2	3	4	5	6	7	8
Amount	$8	$16	$24	$32	$40	$48	$56	$64

According to the data, Tyler would be paid _____ for babysitting $7\frac{1}{2}$ hours.

Original content Copyright © by Houghton Mifflin Harcourt. Additions and changes to the original content are the responsibility of the instructor.

LESSON 14-1

Scatter Plots and Association
Reteach

Many problems involving scatter plots have two parts.

Part I. Make a scatter plot from the following data values.

x	5	7	8	10	12	15	17	20	21	23
y	9	11	10	13	15	17	18	19	19	20

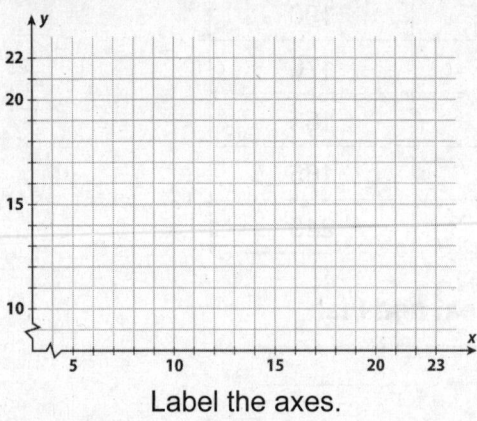
Label the axes.

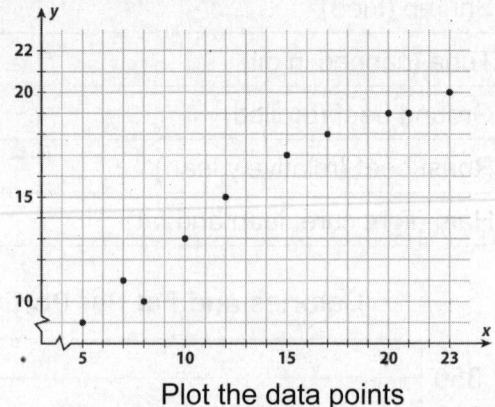
Plot the data points

Part 2. Interpret the scatter plot.

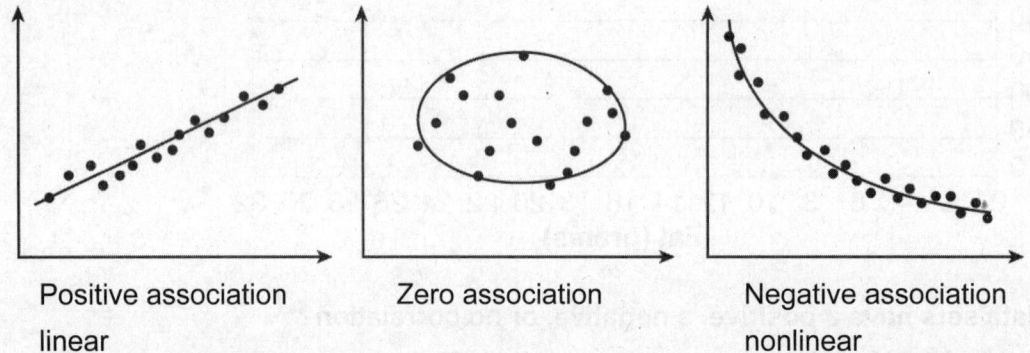

Positive association — linear

Zero association

Negative association — nonlinear

To interpret a scatter plot, data have a *positive association* if the points get higher from left to right. Data have a *negative association* if the points get lower from left to right. Also, the association is *linear* if the points lie along a line. The association is *nonlinear* if the points do not lie along a line.

---

1. Make a scatter plot for the given data. Then interpret the scatter plot.

x	3	5	6	8	9
y	5	5	6	6	8

x	10	12	13	16	17
y	12	15	16	16	15

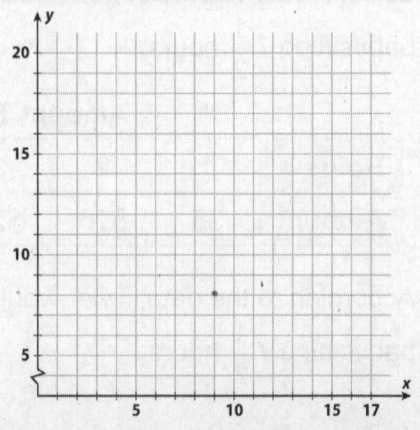

Name _____ Date _____ Class _____

LESSON 14-2
Trend Lines and Predictions
Practice and Problem Solving: A/B

Use the scatter plot for Exercises 1–6.

1. Does the pattern of association between time (number of hours traveled) and distance (number of miles traveled) appear to be linear or nonlinear? Explain.

   _____

   _____

Time and Distance Traveled

2. Explain any clustering.

   _____

3. Identify any possible outliers.

   _____

4. Write an equation for the line of best fit.

   _____

5. What does the slope of the line of best fit represent?

   _____

6. What does the *y*-intercept of the line of best fit represent?

   _____

LESSON 14-2

Trend Lines and Predictions
Reteach

Here is another way to find the equation of a trend line.

Find the equation of a trend line that passes through the points (6, 9) and (12, 13).

Step 1. Find the slope: $m = \dfrac{y_2 - y_1}{x_2 - x_1} = \dfrac{13 - 9}{12 - 6} = \dfrac{4}{6} = \dfrac{2}{3}$

Step 2. Substitute $(x_1, y_1) = (6, 9)$ and $m = \dfrac{2}{3}$ into the equation $y - y_1 = m(x - x_1)$.

$$y - y_1 = m(x - x_1) \rightarrow y - 9 = \dfrac{2}{3}(x - 6)$$

$$y - 9 = \dfrac{2}{3}x - 4$$

$$y = \dfrac{2}{3}x + 5$$

Note: The equation $y - y_1 = m(x - x_1)$ is called the point-slope form of an equation.

Find the equation of the line through each pair of points. Use the equation $y - y_1 = m(x - x_1)$ to find the equation.

1. (4, −10) and (10, −28)

2. (3, −14) and (20, 3)

3. (2, −6) and (20, −15)

4. (1, 6) and (8, 48)

Find the equation of the trend line for the given pair of points. Then use your equation to predict the y value for the given x value.

5. (3, 1) and (24, 15); predict y if x = 15.

6. (3, −8) and (8, −33); predict y if x = 11.

Name _____ Date _____ Class _____

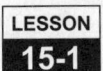

Two-Way Frequency Tables
Practice and Problem Solving: A/B

Complete the table. Then answer the questions that follow.

	Siblings	No Siblings	TOTAL
Boys	12	1. _____	25
Girls	10	14	2. _____
TOTAL	3. _____	4. _____	5. _____

6. What is the relative frequency of selecting a boy?

   _____

7. What is the relative frequency of selecting a boy out of the children who have siblings?

   _____

8. Compare the relative frequencies. Is there an association between being a boy and having siblings? Explain.

   _____

Complete the table. Then answer the questions that follow.

	Blooms	Does Not Bloom	TOTAL
Grows in Shade	75	9. _____	125
Grows in Sunlight	10. _____	85	110
TOTAL	100	11. _____	12. _____

13. What is the relative frequency of selecting a plant that blooms?

    _____

14. Out of plants that grow in the shade, what is the relative frequency of

    selecting one that blooms? _____

15. Compare the relative frequencies. Is there an association between being a plant that blooms and growing in the shade? Explain.

    _____

Original content Copyright © by Houghton Mifflin Harcourt. Additions and changes to the original content are the responsibility of the instructor.

Name _____ Date _____ Class _____

LESSON 15-1 Two-Way Frequency Tables
Reteach

A two-way frequency table allows you to see the relationships among two or more pairs of variables in a real-world situation.

Automobile Fuel Mileage and Commuting Distance

	Mileage < 20 mi/gal	Mileage ≥ 20 mi/gal	TOTAL
3-Mile Commute	18	3	21
30-Mile Commute	5	24	29
TOTAL	23	27	50

Notice that a total value is shown for each column or row, and that the total for the far right column and the bottom row are the same, 50. This is the total number of commuters surveyed.

Looking for an Association The table can show whether there is a relationship between commuting distance and gas mileage.

3-Mile Commute and Mileage

What fraction of commuters drove 3 miles and got 20 miles per gallon or more?

Number who drove 3 miles: **21**

Number of those with mileage ≥ 20 mi/gal: **3**

The fraction is $\frac{3}{21}$, or about 14%.

30-Mile Commute and Mileage

What fraction of commuters drove 30 miles and got 20 miles per gallon or more?

Number who drove 30 miles: **29**

Number of those with mileage ≥ 20 mi/gal: **24**

The fraction is $\frac{24}{29}$, or about 83%.

Use the table above to answer the questions.

1. What association exists between commuters who drove 3 miles and commuters who got **less than** 20 miles per gallon? Use the data in your answer.

   _____

2. What association exists between commuters who drove 30 miles and commuters who got **less than** 20 miles per gallon? Use the data in your answer.

   _____

3. What other factors besides gas mileage should be considered when making an analysis of the costs of commuting 3 miles and 30 miles?

   _____

Original content Copyright © by Houghton Mifflin Harcourt. Additions and changes to the original content are the responsibility of the instructor.

Name _____ Date _____ Class _____

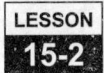

LESSON 15-2 Two-Way Relative Frequency Tables
Practice and Problem Solving: A/B

Rewrite each frequency in the table as a relative frequency. Write each one as a percent to the nearest whole percent. Show your work.

Home Heating Energy Sources Sample

	Electric	Gas	TOTAL
Inside City Limits	35 1. _____	55 2. _____	90 3. _____
Outside City Limits	60 4. _____	15 5. _____	75 6. _____
TOTAL	95 7. _____	70 8. _____	165 9. _____

Complete.

10. Name the four joint relative frequencies (JRFs) shown in the table by using the names of the columns *and* rows. Give the percent for each. Show your work.

    JRF name: _____, _____   percent: _____

    JRF name: _____, _____   percent: _____

    JRF name: _____, _____   percent: _____

    JRF name: _____, _____   percent: _____

11. Name the four marginal relative frequencies (MRFs) in the table by using the name of the column *or* row. Give the percent for each. Show your work.

    MRF name: _____   percent: _____

    MRF name: _____   percent: _____

    MRF name: _____   percent: _____

    MRF name: _____   percent: _____

Calculate the conditional relative frequency.

12. Electric, Inside City Limits: 13. Gas, Outside City Limits:

    _____ ÷ _____ = _____   _____ ÷ _____ ≈ _____

Original content Copyright © by Houghton Mifflin Harcourt. Additions and changes to the original content are the responsibility of the instructor.

Lesson 15-2: Two-Way Relative Frequency Tables
Reteach

Comparison of the different relative frequencies in data can reveal associations or trends that the frequencies themselves might not show.

The table below compares the weights of corn chips found in two different sizes of bags of three brands.

Amount of chips in 24-Ounce Bags

	Bags with less than 24 ounces of chips	Bags with more than 24 ounces of chips	Bags with exactly 24 ounces of chips	TOTAL
Brand A	12	10	40	62
Brand B	9	15	55	79
Brand C	7	6	25	38
TOTAL	28	31	120	179

Marginal Relative Frequency (MRF)

The MRF is a fraction that compares the sum of all frequencies in one row or column to the total of all frequencies of all columns and rows.

Example

Find the MRF of all of Brand A's samples.

$62 \div 179 = 0.35$, or about 35%.

Conditional Relative Frequency (CRF)

The CRF is a fraction that compares one frequency in a row or column to the total of all factors in that row or column.

Example

Find the CRF of Brand A samples with less than 24 ounces of chips.

$12 \div 62 = 0.19$, or about 19%.

Solve. Show your work.

1. Which brand may have quality-control problems when it comes to selling the advertised amount of chips in its 24-ounce bag? Use MRF and/or CRF values to support your answer.

   _____

   _____

   _____

2. Which brand has the greatest CRF for **less than** the advertised weight of chips? What does this indicate about the accuracy of its label?

   _____